INDEPENDENTLY WEALTHY

How to Build Financial Security in the New Economic Era

ROBERT GOODMAN, Ph.D.

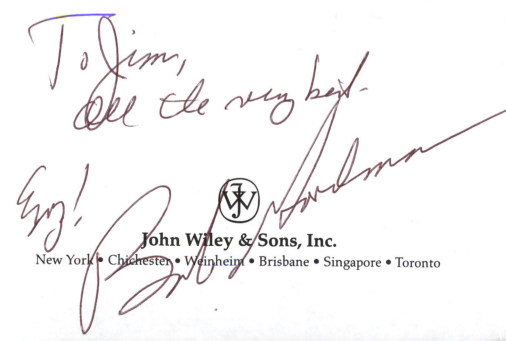

John Wiley & Sons, Inc.

New York • Chichester • Weinheim • Brisbane • Singapore • Toronto

Library of Congress Cataloging-in-Publication Data:
Goodman, Robert, 1941—
    Independently wealthy : how to build financial security in the new
economic era / Robert Goodman.
        p.   cm.
    Includes index.
    ISBN 0-471-19244-9 (alk. paper)
        1. Finance, Personal.   2. Investments.   3. Financial security.
I. Title
HG179.G678   1996
332.024—dc20   96-12271
                                                    CIP

Printed in the United States of America

10   9   8   7   6   5   4   3   2   1

TO MERI,

MY INSPIRATION

ACKNOWLEDGMENTS

This book would not have been written had it not been for the suggestion and insistence of Larry Chambers, an author and financial journalist. Larry provided the encouragement and advice that proved to be the catalyst for moving this project from concept to keyboard.

I wish to thank Bill Shiebler, Senior Managing Director of Putnam Investments, for his constant support throughout this undertaking, and for his unwavering, unflagging faith that this task could be accomplished on time and in good shape.

My colleague Susan Feldman has earned my gratitude for plenty of on-call hand-holding as this project moved forward, and for her skillful handling of the negotiations that are inevitable with this type of production.

In addition, I am immensely grateful to Pamela van Giessen, my editor at John Wiley & Sons, for her insight, advice, and expertise throughout the entire publishing process.

Finally, I am especially indebted to my colleague and friend, Ron Mills. His influence is so pervasive that it is impossible to credit fairly. His insight, editorial and writing skills, and grasp of the material are marked on every page of this book.

CONTENTS

Part II
Taking Charge of Your Financial Future   71

Chapter 5
The Key to Wealth   73

Saving versus Investing
Risk: Perception versus Reality
The Risk of "Playing It Safe"
Market Risk: Savers Beware
What Is Ownership?
It's Time in the Market, Not Timing the Market
Common Stocks: A Piece of the Action
The Importance of a Long-term Commitment
Understanding Your Choices
Growth Stocks
Value Stocks
Income Stocks
Risk: No Pain, No Gain

Chapter 6
The Path to Wealth   95

Planning Your Voyage
Finding the Right Financial Advisor: Choose Carefully
Ask for References
Check Credentials
Ask How the Advisor Is Paid
Make Sure the Advisor Can Serve Your Goals
Look for Compatibility
You Are in Charge
Setting Your Goals and Objectives
Building Your Capital Base
Dollar-cost Averaging: The Eighth Wonder of the World
The Magic of Compounding
Managing the Risks
Invest Regularly

FOREWORD

Bob Goodman has a way of breathing life into the arcane science of economics for the noneconomists among us, whether he is on the road carrying his message to the public or on one of his rare trips back here in Boston to update his colleagues. For the past three years, his major theme has been that times are changing and each of us must change with them if we are to have a financially secure future. It is an important message and I am pleased that he has undertaken the task of putting it into print.

Growing up in the Boston of the '30s and '40s, in a family with a strong heritage in the law and money management, I learned early the importance of developing a disciplined approach to saving and investing. From the day I began receiving an allowance, my father strongly suggested that I put a portion aside for the future. It was not easy, because my father was not overly generous in determining the amount I should receive. However, if at the end of a year, I actually had available money saved from my allowance or modest earnings, he would match it for investment.

When I entered the investment management business my-self in the early 1950s, our country was just beginning what would become a virtually uninterrupted forty-year period of economic growth. Millions of Americans who had lost their savings in the stock market crash and subsequent bank clo-sures, endured the deprivations of the Great Depression, and fought in the war against fascism stood on the edge of a future that held great promise—and great uncertainty. They also faced that future with the typical optimism and vigor for which Americans have always been known.

The United States was founded by people with a strong com-mitment to self-reliance and the freedom to make choices for themselves. It was built upon the solid foundation of a free-market economy. As it prospered and grew, a social fabric was woven around the precepts of economic justice and opportunity for all. As you will be reminded in this important new book, a free-market economy and economic equality are not always compatible. What makes our country work is its enduring abil-ity to maintain a delicate balance between the two. Sometimes the pendulum swings in favor of one, sometimes in favor of the other. But no matter how long these swings may be, the pendu-lum never stops moving.

As millions of workers began contributing to the prosperity of the '50s and '60s, in typically American fashion, they de-manded a share. Much of what they received came in the form of retirement benefits—pensions from their employers and in-creased Social Security payments and Medicare from the fed-eral government. Employers' automatic contributions to pen-sion plans and the generous benefits from the government obviated the need for workers to make serious investments in their own future financial security. As a result, all too many of them got out of the habit of saving and investing—or never de-veloped the habit at all.

Even more worrisome, as a people we came to view these government benefits as "entitlements," something that was due us. Few listened to the warnings of those who dared to call attention to what should have been obvious: the country could not afford to provide such largesse indefinitely. Because it was popular to do so, our politicians kept giving us what we told them we wanted, putting off the tough decisions that would only become tougher with the passage of time.

Now we have begun to send our politicians a different message. The first reversal in the balance of power in Congress in four decades after the 1994 elections was a clear signal that the next great swing of the pendulum may have begun. We have already seen a significant shift in how corporate America is approaching the way it handles retirement planning for its employees. Instead of setting aside money for pensions managed as one pool from which all employee retirement benefits will be drawn, it is becoming common practice for employers to create plans under which employees must make their own decisions as to how what will eventually be their retirement money is invested. This is both an opportunity and a challenge, since the quality of life in retirement will be affected by investment decisions individuals must make during their working years.

Whatever your politics, you must understand what this and other important new trends mean for America—and for you. In his inimitable way, Bob tells you what it means. Ever the optimist, he does not view the future darkly. Rather, he sees it as one of great promise for those who are able to recognize the opportunities that will open up before them and have the knowledge, discipline, and self-reliance to take advantage of them.

—GEORGE PUTNAM
Chairman, The Putnam Funds
Boston, April 1996

"*I find the great thing in this world is not so much where we stand, as in what direction we are moving. To reach the port of heaven, we must sail sometimes with the wind and sometimes against it—but we must sail, and not drift, nor lie at anchor.*"

—OLIVER WENDELL HOLMES, *The Autocrat of the Breakfast Table*, 1858

SETTING SAIL IN ROUGH FINANCIAL WATERS

*I must go down to the seas again
to the lonely sea and the sky.
And all I ask is a tall ship
and a star to steer her by. . . .*
—JOHN MASEFIELD, 1902

Imagine you are traveling on a large ship. You wake up one morning and realize there is no captain, no crew. Just you alone. A storm is raging and you desperately need to find a port. All the equipment is aboard, all the tools necessary to guide the ship are available. But you lack the knowledge and skill to navigate safely.

This scenario is not unlike the situation now facing millions of Americans as they desperately try to achieve financial security. Cast adrift in a sea of financial confusion, they feel powerless, unable to control their financial destinies.

The purpose of this book is threefold:

- To explain clearly and understandably the nature of our economic system; what it can do and what it cannot do.

- To clarify the major financial problems and the unique investment opportunities that lie ahead of us as we enter the twenty-first century.
- To provide a guide that can help you set your course for financial independence.

Before developing a coherent financial plan, it is imperative that you understand how the political, economic, and financial worlds interrelate and interact—and you must gain this understanding regardless of your personal political and philosophical leanings.

As we will see, the economic realities now confronting our policymakers are forcing them to develop policies that will fly in the face of our political and economic experience. The American people are being sent a clear, yet unspoken message.

Regardless of your age and stage of life, you should assume that the government will not be there to help you in the ways you have come to expect. Instead of Uncle Sam dispensing funds directly to the people, responsibility for providing for individual income needs will gradually and subtly be shifted to each of us. Virtually every working American will be affected by the coming changes. Those aged 40 and under will be on their own when they reach retirement age. For those who are older, longer life expectancy means retirement years that could equal the number of years of work.

Social Security cannot continue to exist in its present form. Neither can Medicare, Medicaid, or welfare. These and other "entitlements," heretofore politically sacrosanct, will be dramatically altered, reduced, or eliminated. The handwriting is on the wall: to live a financially secure life in this changing economic environment, you will need a much larger nest egg than did any prior generation. A clear understanding of the serious nature of this challenge is essential if you are to become financially independent.

If you have not already begun the process of accumulating the assets you will need to assure such independence, you should start now. But before you can venture forth on your own savings and investment program, you'll need some navigational aids—a compass and charts.

By the time you finish reading this book, you will have your compass and charts in hand. You will have gained an insight into the political and economic realities that surround us each day, and you will know the mistakes most savers and investors make so you can avoid them. Finally, you will learn how to construct a detailed financial plan that works.

Once gained, this knowledge will give you confidence to chart your course and make the necessary adjustments along the way. With everything you need on board, and with this book providing your compass and charts, you may even be able to sit back and enjoy the voyage.

PART I

THE RELUCTANT
CAPITALISTS

CHAPTER 1

THE ENDURING CONFLICT:
ECONOMIC EFFICIENCY
VERSUS ECONOMIC JUSTICE

"I know of no country, indeed, where the love of money has taken stronger hold on the affections of men and where a profounder contempt is expressed for the theory of the permanent equality of property."
—ALEXIS DE TOQUEVILLE, *Democracy in America*, 1835

EXAMINING THE ROOTS
OF THE CONFLICT

Perhaps the failure of many investors to achieve financial security stems from the fact that Americans are reluctant capitalists; that is, we desire all the benefits that a capitalistic free-enterprise system provides, without the costs. As we will see, the benefits and costs are inextricably bound together. To set a course for successful investing, it is imperative that we distinguish between the economic and the social consequences of economic policy.

This distinction is made difficult because as Americans, we have had a long-standing love affair with a four-letter word that begins with "F." We use it every day to describe everything from our social values to our legal statutes. The word is "fair." Typically, we use the word as if it had but one meaning. Practically speaking, however, the definition will differ depending on whether we are referring to our notion of economic justice or economic efficiency. Making the distinction is essential if we are to put into perspective the seeming conflict between the outcome of free-market economics and our desire for economic equality.

When referring to economic justice, fair implies freedom from self-interest, prejudice, or favoritism—evenhandedness. When referring to economic efficiency, however, another meaning is more appropriate: conforming with established rules. Thus, when defining our notion of economic justice, the word addresses the quality of a predetermined outcome; when referring to an efficiently functioning economy, fair means that, as long as we follow the established rules, whatever outcome is obtained from the dynamics of the system is considered just.

The fact is, a free-market economic system is blind. It does not care whether you are male or female, short or tall, old or young. All the system was designed to do was to provide the most output at the least cost. It will distribute goods and services in an economically efficient manner. It is important to emphasize that this does not necessarily mean it will distribute these goods and services in a socially desirable way.

Capitalism makes no interpersonal comparisons nor moral judgments. It is amoral. Our worth, or value to the system, is determined solely by the extent of our contribution to the output of the system. You can be the kindest, gentlest, most considerate individual on earth, but if you do not produce something or contribute something to the overall production of goods and services, you have no economic value. Economically speaking, you are worthless. Conversely, you may be a serial killer, but if you produce marketable goods or services, you have value.

These are harsh statements, but they are true. They may fly in the face of everything you learned at home, in school, or in your place of worship. But, like it or not, understanding the nature of our economic system is the first step in developing the mind-set to deal effectively with your financial affairs.

Let me illustrate. When used to describe the efficient functioning of our economic system, fair means that if you produce five dollars' worth of goods and services in an hour, you should receive five dollars of income for that hour of work. If you produce one hundred dollars' worth of goods and services in an hour, you should receive an hourly income of one hundred dollars. For our economic system to operate efficiently, then, each of us must earn enough income to buy back what we have produced. No more, no less. In fact, to the extent that all individuals are not equally productive, the efficient functioning of an economy *requires* income inequality.

In a freely functioning capitalistic society, we must produce in order to consume. The only way we will be able to consume is if we produce something of value. Under our free-market system, if allowed to operate unfettered, 20 percent of the population could wind up with 80 percent of the output if the same 20 percent had been responsible for 80 percent of the production. In an efficiently functioning economy, over time, the fruits of economic growth will accrue only to those who produced that growth and in proportion to their contribution to it. The outcome of a free-market system will not be evenhanded.

Fair as a synonym for economic justice is used to describe the allocation of goods and services based upon need, irrespective of whether the level of goods and services is representative of the individual's productive contribution. In effect, a portion of income is redistributed from those who produce it to those who consume it. Typically, this result is achieved through tax policy. The object of policy becomes the reduction of the disparities between income levels created by market forces. Examples of such redistributive programs are welfare, unemployment and workers' compensation, and rent, crop, and food subsidies. While the objective of these programs is highly laudable and reflective of the American spirit, their implementation may very well impede the ability of the economy to operate at its most efficient level.

CAPITALISM AND DEMOCRACY: OIL AND WATER

At this juncture, it is important that I make my point of view crystal clear. I believe government does have an important role to play in economic matters. Government should provide an environment in which corporations and individuals can pursue their legitimate economic objectives efficiently. Some governmental control is necessary to protect us from the evils of monopoly. Providing for the national defense, fair-labor practices, and taxation are all legitimate governmental functions.

The challenge is to work out a system whereby we can improve the workings of a less-than-perfect competitive system. As Paul Samuelson, the Nobel-prize-winning economist, has said, "The relevant choice for policy today is not a decision between the extremes of laissez-faire and totalitarian dictatorship of production, but rather the degree to which public policy should do less or more in modifying the operation of particular private economic activities." The more efficiently an economy is allowed to operate, the more growth will be achieved, and an economic environment will be created in which each individual will be able to achieve his or her potential.

As we will see later, when the economic philosophy of our government tends to emphasize the redistribution of income away from the direction in which it would naturally flow, the economic environment becomes increasingly inefficient, growth slows, productivity stagnates, interest rates and inflation rise sharply, resources are misallocated, and financial markets do poorly. Conversely, during periods when the government advocates policies that allow markets to move freely and enhance the desirability of saving, investing, and producing, the economy responds with vigor, inflation and interest rates decline, and the financial markets, reflecting economic health, respond favorably.

Predictably, each of these situations will set forces in motion that ultimately trigger a reaction. For example, the threat of a collapsing economy will lead to the adoption of policies designed to save it. After its rescue, as the more productive segments of society get ahead faster than the less productive (a predictable outcome), and as income disparities between these groups widen, the unevenness of the results of economic freedom comes back into focus and, in a political system where the majority rules, the people will vote to change direction.

The conclusion to which one is led is disturbing—that capitalism and democracy are, by their very nature, incompatible. To satisfy the objective of one system may—and often does—preclude achieving the objectives of the other. Perhaps the systems could work better together if we could accept the notion that a mechanic may have a lower standard of living than a neurosurgeon and a neurosurgeon may have a lower standard of living than a rock star.

You might ask why a rock star is worth more on the economic ladder than a neurosurgeon. The answer is simple: because the market says so. The interaction of the supply of and demand for goods and services represents the decisions of literally millions of individuals. The market value of work is determined by its productivity, irrespective of who produces it. In this sense, the economic value of a product or service may differ from its social value.

While it is true that many factors enter into this determination, the marketplace is highly impersonal, and the result of market forces may not square with our own individual preferences or personal value systems. For example, when those collective decisions create a huge demand for a certain rock star's music and relatively less for neurosurgery, the rock star will command more money than a neurosurgeon. We should remember, however, that the average neurosurgeon still earns more than the average rock musician.

As individuals, we must take market-determined results as a given. While this may seem defeatist, it is realistic. We live in a world governed by the laws of supply and demand. To try to change this reality would be like tilting at windmills. We must understand this reality and then deal with it. Remember, there is no moral standard in the marketplace. When it comes to successful investing, and as much as it might go against the grain, we must see the world the way it is, not the way we would like it to be. Unfortunately, dissatisfaction with the social implications of economic policy may be among the major distractions that prevent investors from making appropriate investment decisions.

ECONOMIC GYROSCOPE: THE INEXORABLE QUEST FOR EQUILIBRIUM

No matter how hard we try to force our economic system to be evenhanded in a social sense through the redistribution of resources and output, the economic system will work against us in an attempt to restore market efficiency and equilibrium. A perfect example is the cruel hoax of the minimum wage. In an admirable attempt to help individuals at the lower end of the income ladder, we have instituted the concept of a minimum wage rate that will give people a minimum standard of living— a "living wage," as it is often put.

In 1956, the minimum wage was $1.00 an hour. In 1995, it was $4.25. One is tempted to conclude that individuals earning the minimum wage in 1995 were more than four times better off than those earning this wage in 1956. However, when we give individuals more purchasing power than is represented by their production, we do not increase the amount of goods and services available. We have only increased the number of dollars chasing the same quantity of goods and services. Over time, that leads to higher prices and ultimately removes any advantage the increase bestowed. The economic system will try to take back from them that which they did not produce.

Unless minimum-wage workers have become more productive over time, economic theory suggests that they will be able to buy as much as—and no more than—they could buy before. In fact, after adjusting for price increases since 1956, today's $4.25 per hour will buy what a dollar per hour bought 40 years ago. Despite all of society's well-intentioned efforts, it has not been able to increase this group's command over goods and services.

We do not have to constrain ourselves by looking only at the minimum wage to see how these forces work over time. Figure 1.1 illustrates the validity of the notion that the only way workers in general can improve their standard of living is by increasing their productivity. When they do not become more productive, any increase in their hourly wage will ultimately be taken away by inflation.

The most comprehensive and internally consistent set of statistics we have on the subject is the series produced by the Bureau of Labor Statistics. The figures cover the hours of work of all people engaged in the business sector, including the hours of proprietors and unpaid family workers. Their compensation includes fringe benefits and an estimate of wages, salaries, and supplemental payments for the self-employed.

By adjusting the hourly compensation reported in this series for the price of the totality of the output that the business sector produces, we can see how much of their own product workers can buy with the compensation for an hour's work. If we take 1950 as a base, we see that by the end of 1994, real compensation had tracked productivity very closely throughout the entire 44-year period. Figure 1.1 shows how, over time, the congruence of the index of real compensation and the index of productivity is nearly perfect.

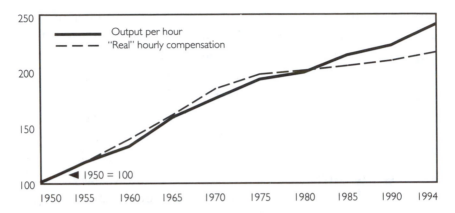

FIGURE 1.1 Regardless of how far or how fast workers' paychecks may rise, their real purchasing power will be determined by how much their productivity improves. Only when productivity rises can workers enjoy real gains in purchasing power. (Source: U.S. Department of Labor, Bureau of Labor Statistics)

The conclusion is inescapable: over long periods, real purchasing power will conform to productivity growth. The growth in real wages and worker command over goods and services is inextricably tied to the ability of workers to increase their productive capabilities. Of course, individual workers can forge ahead of the pack by raising the amount of their individual output. Again, the rewards of production will be commensurate with the value of the product.

This relationship suggests that attempts by government to alter the income distribution between groups of workers manifesting different rates of productivity growth, over the long run, will be destined to meet with failure. Real compensation for each group ultimately will depend upon that group's contribution to the overall growth of output.

THE ECONOMIC PENDULUM SWINGS SLOWLY

Our political system reflects our social values. We all count the same—one person, one vote—regardless of our contribution to overall production. Consequently, since the definition of economic justice, or what is fair, conflicts with the definition of economic efficiency, a tug-of-war becomes inevitable. This struggle between a political system seeking to allocate output in a socially desirable way and an economic system constantly attempting to utilize resources in the most efficient and productive manner gives rise to relatively long cycles that manifest profoundly different economic and investment conditions. Like a large pendulum, the slow oscillations between these policy cycles will persist as long as we have a free-market economic system working within a democracy.

As we will examine in greater detail later, successfully meeting your long-term investment objectives requires that you be able to discern these subtle shifts in economic philosophy. If you do, you will be able to position your assets appropriately. Short-term movements of the business cycle can, and often do, obscure these more important longer-term trends. Your ability to distinguish between the economy's short-term cyclical movements and the longer-term trends is a crucial element in establishing your long-term investment plan and sticking to it.

CHAPTER 2

THE KEYNESIAN REVOLUTION AND THE CONCEPT OF ECONOMIC JUSTICE

"The central controls necessary to ensure full-employment, of course, will involve a large extension of the traditional functions of government."
—JOHN MAYNARD KEYNES, *General Theory of Employment, Interest and Money,* 1936

ECONOMIC TAILSPIN

It is important for investors always to keep in mind that long-term movements in common stock values ultimately reflect the health of the country's economy—good and bad. And it is always the economic policies pursued by the government that determine the economic environment in which investors must make their investment decisions. As we will see, when the government adopts economic policies that are appropriate for solving our economic problems, the economic environment can become highly conducive to equity investing and the accumulation of wealth. For whatever reasons, however, if economic policies are oriented in the wrong direction or are applied inappropriately, the economic environment will become hostile to investors, and the attainment of investment objectives will become more difficult.

As with any discipline, an understanding of history provides a good foundation on which to put current events into their proper perspective. From an economic point of view, the Great Depression of the 1930s seems an appropriate place to begin our discussion. Economists and historians may disagree over the precise causes of that depression, but what seems clear is that a confluence of unfortunate policy decisions led to the collapse of the U.S. economy. Contrary to popular opinion, the stock market crash of 1929 was not the cause of the depression. Rather, it was merely reflective of an economic environment that was becoming increasingly more dangerous as a result of misguided economic policy. The economy was already slipping into recession when the crash occurred in October.

At that time, the United States was operating under a gold standard in which the rules of the game required that when a country was experiencing an outflow of capital it should raise interest rates. The idea was to make domestic investments more attractive to investors so they would not send their capital elsewhere. Playing by those rules, the Federal Reserve Board kept raising interest rates. Instead of spurring investment, however, the action only depressed economic activity further. For the next 18 months, in fact, the Fed kept raising rates—and economic activity kept slowing. Ultimately, inappropriate monetary policy worsened an already deteriorating economic situation.

In an attempt to restart the economic engine by bolstering demand for domestic goods, Congress passed the Smoot-Hawley Act in June 1930. Retaliation by the country's trading partners to the act's 50 percent tariff on all imported goods was swift and certain; the U.S. economy virtually collapsed.

During the depression that spanned the entire decade of the 1930s, conditions became so desperate that people who were working and thus still earning money were so afraid of losing their jobs that they saved most of their income rather than pumping it back into the economy. Because of their restrained spending, the demand for goods and services continued to fall, forcing businesses to close their doors and their employees to lose their jobs. This vicious cycle threw the economy into a tailspin.

The prevailing economic theory suggested that monetary policy was the solution to the malaise: by manipulating interest rates, the government could speed or slow the economy as required to maintain a healthy and sustainable pace. So, instead of raising interest rates—which clearly had not worked—policymakers began lowering them. They reasoned that the lower rates would entice individuals and businesses to borrow money, which they would then spend and invest, and the economic imbalance would right itself.

By the time the Federal Reserve Board undertook its desperate campaign to lower interest rates, consumers and businesses were so depressed that no matter how low rates were pushed, individuals and companies could not be lured into borrowing money to spend. To illustrate how far rates had fallen, by 1935 three-month Treasury bills were yielding less than one-quarter of 1 percent. Still the private sector failed to respond. This situation, which later became known as a *liquidity trap*, would ultimately plague most of the industrialized world for most of the decade.

As demand fell, businesses became ever more desperate to stay viable. They continued to cut the prices of their products in their quest to maintain market share. As a consequence, the United States experienced the rare phenomenon of *deflation*, a situation in which the average price level actually declines. During the period 1929 to 1932, the price level dropped by 24 percent. In 1932 alone, the decline was 10 percent. Corporate profitability fell drastically as these price declines magnified revenue losses from critically low sales volume. In response to these economic conditions, the stock market, as represented by the Dow Jones Industrial Average, fell from its high of 386 in September 1929 to a low of 41 by July 1932, a decline of about 80 percent in value.

In 1930, John Maynard Keynes, the distinguished British economist, had sought unsuccessfully in his *Treatise on Money* to explain why economies operate unevenly and do not always self-correct when interest rates are lowered. The more Keynes thought about the problem and the more he observed the economic crises swirling around him in the United States and Europe as the 1930s unfolded, the more convinced he became that it was indeed possible for an economy to degenerate into a position where there was no automatic tendency for it to recover.

I would like to pause here for a moment to reiterate what I said at the very beginning of this book. My intention is not to make a case for any political or ideological point of view. It is not to defend or attack any action taken or not taken in the twists and turns of history. It is, simply, to place historical events and economic theories in the context of today's environment so we can make what we can only hope will be wise judgments to prepare us well for the future. Like it or not, we must play the hand that history deals us.

GOVERNMENT AS SAVIOR

By 1932, with a quarter of the workforce unemployed and no viable self-correcting mechanism in place, the situation in the United States clearly had become intolerable. If democracy was to survive, a solution had to be found, and found quickly. It could not wait for Keynes to put his theories on paper.

Exercising what Keynes would later take as a basic precept in his theories, the government got into the act early in 1933 by creating spending programs that would pump money directly into the hands of the unemployed. Washington launched huge public works programs to construct dams, bridges, roads, and public buildings. It paid architects and engineers to design the projects. It employed millions of people to build them. To be sure, many of these projects were worthwhile since they improved the infrastructure. But a significant portion of the expenditures represented nothing more than paying someone to dig a hole, then paying someone else to fill it up.

Such "make-work" did not really matter to the government. The object of the policy, remember, was to get money into circulation so it could be spent. This spending would represent income to other individuals and would create further demand for goods and services that people, at work once more, could afford to buy.

One way for the government to increase aggregate demand was through the direct purchase of goods and services from the private sector. If this spending exceeded tax revenues and a budget deficit resulted, so be it. Deficit spending was seen as an indispensable tool to revitalize a depressed economy. The reasoning was that if people were put back to work and profitability returned to corporate America, tax revenues would increase. At "full employment," the budget would be restored to balance. Similarly, during periods of excess demand, budget surpluses would act as a depressant to relieve inflationary pressures. Budget imbalances, therefore, were seen as transitory and of no material consequence to long-term economic stability.

A LONG WALK ON THE DEMAND-SIDE

Observing how the governments of the United States and Great Britain were working to extricate themselves from a deep depression, Keynes published his *General Theory of Employment, Interest and Money* in 1936. This landmark book asserted that, unlike briefer and milder economic recessions, which tended to be self-correcting, depressions did not. It was possible, in fact, for the economy to remain in a state of equilibrium with large numbers of people unemployed, Keynes said. He offered an explanation for this phenomenon, then proposed a solution for it.

Basically, Keynes said that if individuals will not spend money to consume and businesses will not invest in new plant and equipment, and if monetary policy had become impotent to deal with this situation through interest rate manipulation, the government must inject itself directly into the economic system and do it for them. He identified an economy's main problem in such a situation as a lack of demand. Keynes implicitly assumed that there was no binding constraint on an economy's ability to produce goods and services. What was needed was someone to consume what the economy was capable of delivering. In short, it was a problem that needed to be solved by what we have come to call *demand-side* policies.

Keynesian economic policy can be illustrated by comparing it to holding a match to a wet leaf. The match represents the government, the flame is the policies, and the wet leaf is the economy's private sector. If you can hold the match to the leaf long enough, the leaf will dry out and ultimately catch fire, then continue burning by itself.

Another method advocated by Keynes to stimulate aggregate demand was an indirect approach using tax policy. For example, if you were a policymaker and your objective was to stimulate consumer spending, traditional economic theory prescribed a general reduction in income taxes. Keynes recommended a somewhat different approach. He reasoned that it would make more sense to give the bulk of any tax cut to those individuals who could be counted on to spend the greatest proportion of it. Economic theory suggests (and data consistently confirm) that the higher your income, the higher the likelihood that you will tend to save a portion of any increase in that income after taxes. Individuals at the lower end of the income ladder, of necessity, typically spend most, if not all, of their income.

Keynes recommended that to stimulate aggregate demand, the bulk of any income tax reduction should be aimed toward individuals at the lower end of the income stream. A $10 billion tax cut for wealthy individuals might result in only an $8 billion increase in consumption (they would save $2 billion); whereas, the same reduction in taxes for lower-income individuals might be expected to result in the entire tax cut being spent.

It is important to note here that Keynes's initial objective was to solve the problem of underemployment. He was interested only in creating the economic conditions that would provide jobs for all those capable and willing to work. Each individual would ultimately be employed and earn a wage reflective of his or her productive capabilities. As an economist, therefore, Keynes was interested in increasing economic efficiency. Only at full employment, he believed, would this objective be realized.

Nevertheless, as time would demonstrate, only a small gap would separate the Keynesian quest for economic efficiency from the political philosophy of manipulating the system to achieve social objectives in the name of economic justice. Indeed, Keynes himself may have set the stage for the short leap when he wrote in 1936, "For my own part, I believe that there is a social or psychological justification for significant inequalities of incomes and wealth, but not for such large disparities as exist today." And, near the end of his book, the economist recommended his new theory as a rationale for correcting the seeming arbitrary and inequitable distribution of income and wealth that derived from a free-market, capitalistic economic system.

Ironically, Keynes saw his new theory as being moderately conservative in its implications. Again quoting from Keynes: "For whilst it indicates the vital importance of establishing certain central controls in matters which are now left in the main to individual initiative, there are wide fields of activity which are unaffected. The State will have to exercise a guiding influence on the propensity to consume partly through its scheme of taxation, partly by fixing the rate of interest, and partly perhaps in other ways."

But foremost, the economy had to be set back in motion. If you have ever had to push a stalled automobile, you are familiar with Newton's first law of motion: a body at rest tends to stay at rest and a body in motion tends to remain in motion unless, in either case, it is acted upon by an outside force. The law can apply to economics as well as physics. Finally, with the help of massive infusions of federal money, the huge economic machine that was the United States economy began to creak and groan into forward motion.

The economic policies developed and honed during the 1930s worked because they were appropriate for the problem at hand. The *pump-priming* philosophy was effective because it used demand-oriented policies for a demand-side problem. The solution to recession was to pump up demand. Should the economy overheat and inflation accelerate, the policy solution called for dampening demand to reduce the pressure. For decades following the depression, the government promoted economic growth by manipulating demand through the use of monetary and fiscal policies. This direct intervention of government into the economic system led to a sequence of events where the government's monetary and fiscal policymakers would pump up demand and then retard it. Pump and retard. Pump and retard.

Even as Washington bent to the task of getting the country's industry back on track, government leaders realized that America's labor force also needed a support system built under it. There were three legs to the structure that finally emerged. The first was to raise employment which, as I have said, was accomplished largely through ambitious public works and public spending programs. The second was to strengthen the position of organized labor. The government's leaders reasoned that without strong labor walking alongside strong industry, past abuses would only be repeated and ultimately lead to ugly, painful, and costly confrontations like those that had marked the labor movement in the nineteenth and early twentieth centuries. The third leg was to improve the economic security of workers through a system of unemployment insurance, old-age insurance, and wage-and-hour laws.

THE CONCEPT OF SAFETY NETS

The Railroad Retirement Act of 1935 was the first of these safety nets. A precursor of Social Security, it directed the federal government to administer the pensions of railroad workers based on taxes levied equally on workers' wages and employers' payrolls.

The Fair Labor Standards Act of 1938, more popularly known as the Wages and Hours Act, built a floor under wages and placed a ceiling on weekly hours of work. It applied to workers in all businesses engaged in interstate commerce. The legislation imposed a minimum wage of 25 cents an hour in the first year (1939), rising to 40 cents an hour over seven years. Even by the standards of the time, this was hardly a "living wage," nor was it ever intended to be. The minimum wage in concept and execution was considered a helping hand to those who found themselves in temporary economic distress. The hourly rate was raised to 75 cents in 1949 and $1.00 in 1956 (see Table 2.1).

The Social Security Act of 1935 began modestly enough; the first step in its implementation was to create a nationwide pension system for needy persons 65 and over. The federal government matched state funds dollar for dollar to a $20 maximum monthly limit. Phase two was the contributory old-age plan that forms the basis of Social Security as we know it today. Then, as now, it was funded by a tax on employees' incomes and employers' payrolls. Then, as now, the tax revenues from current workers supported eligible retirees. It was never intended as a primary pension plan.

TABLE 2.1 Minimum Wages (1939–1995)

Effective date	Minimum rate for nonfarm workers	Effective date	Minimum rate for nonfarm workers
1939	$0.25	1975	$2.10
1946	0.40	1978	2.65
1950	0.75	1979	2.90
1956	1.00	1980	3.10
1963	1.25	1981	3.35
1967	1.40	1990	3.80
1968	1.60	1991	4.25
1974	2.00	1995	4.25
			(no change since 1991)

(Source: World Almanac)

WAR AND POSTWAR RECOVERY FUEL THE ECONOMIC ENGINE

As the 1930s gave way to the 1940s, the economy began to gain substantial momentum. Thanks in no small part to the mobilization effort leading up to and during World War II, the economy of the '40s approached full utilization of the labor force. At war's end, pent-up consumer demand for goods and services was unleashed. Concern that returning veterans would flood the labor market and swell the jobless rolls proved short-lived. Aggregate demand was further fueled by growing need abroad for U.S. goods as the rest of the world recovered from the ravages of war.

The world's ability to sate this appetite was due in large part to one of history's happy confluences of political and economic interests. The Marshall Plan, known officially as the European Recovery Program, was put forth by U.S. Secretary of State George C. Marshall in a 1947 speech at Harvard University. Drawing an important lesson from history, Secretary Marshall declared that instead of imposing reparations upon the foe, as had been done following World War I, the victors should help the vanquished enemy back onto its feet.

Between 1948 and 1951, the United States pumped economic aid into Europe to the tune of some $12.5 billion in grants and loans, a sum almost staggering to comprehend at the time. Europe, including Germany, soon was not only back on its feet, but thriving. Factories had been rebuilt, roads, rail lines, and bridges repaired or replaced. In cities, new buildings quickly rose from the rubble of war. The recovery in Germany was so swift and complete that it became known as the "economic miracle."

Washington took the same approach in the Pacific following Japan's surrender, though the process was somewhat more challenging. At war's end, Japan had practically no capability for domestic food production, and industrial capacity was essentially wiped out. Again, however, with the help of substantial amounts of U.S. aid, economic recovery was rapid. Despite the fast pace of recovery in Europe and Japan, its cost was not met with universal acclaim at home. Critics decried the amount of aid Washington was extending to the nation's former enemies.

Washington's worry over a return to depression following the war had created a hidden agenda—and, in the end, provided a major boost to the country's economy. The Marshall Plan and other aid programs were seen as a way of sustaining the demand for U. S. goods. Indeed, more than half of the $12.5 billion in aid to Europe was used to purchase U.S.–manufactured machinery, steel, and other construction materials, business and office products, and consumer goods of all descriptions. Most of the food required to sustain Japan's populace immediately after war's end came from American farms. As in Europe, American industry played a major role in restoring Japan's virtually nonexistent productive capability. America's huge capacity to produce, which had been indispensable in winning the global war, had become essential in recovering from it.

BABY BOOMERS: WAR'S LASTING LEGACY

Pent-up demand created by the war was not confined to consumer goods. Between 1946 and 1964, babies arrived in num-

bers not seen before or since. The generational bulge of "baby-
boomers"—76 million strong—will be working its way through
life's stages until well into the twenty-first century, creating
huge and changing economic implications not only for themselves but for those who precede them and those who follow in
their wake.

Throughout the three decades following World War II, U.S.
economic policy remained focused on managing demand.
Meanwhile, the country was slowly and inexorably falling behind in its ability to fulfill that demand. It simply was not expanding plant and equipment rapidly enough to produce everything consumers wanted.

TAXES AS TOOLS FOR SHAPING POLICY

While the Keynesian revolution provided the policy solution to
the economic problem of the 1930s, it also provided the rationale that would later be used to justify using the tax system as a
tool for pursuing economic justice. Tax policy was seen as a
mechanism that could be manipulated by the government to
achieve social objectives. In the name of economic justice,
policymakers believed that for "fairness," marginal income tax
rates should be progressively higher as income levels rose.
They saw making tax rates progressive as a way of redistribut-
ing income from higher-income earners to lower-income earners. They argued that the general welfare would be improved if
incomes were more evenly distributed and income disparities
were reduced. I will demonstrate later why this assumption
may not always be valid.

Meanwhile, during the 1950s and through the mid-1960s,
economic policies remained appropriate for fostering economic
growth. While the objective of establishing and maintaining full
employment remained elusive, corporate profitability, reflecting
stable prices and high productivity, was on the upswing. From
1961 through 1968, in fact, Congress, at the behest of the White

House, pursued deliberate policies of running budgetary deficits in order to avoid sluggishness in the economy.

As Keynesian theory would suggest, the expansionary effect of the budget deficits served to offset a deflationary bias in the economy. Productivity was growing strongly during this period. Inflation remained remarkably low, running at a 1 percent to 2 percent annual rate. Interest rates varied little and had settled at levels conducive to productive borrowing. As it inevitably does, the stock market reflected the prevailing economic and government policy environment. Even accounting for cyclical variations in stock prices between 1954 and 1966, the Dow Jones Industrial Average rose from 250 to 1000—a fourfold increase in 12 years.

The escalation of the war in Vietnam and the simultaneous undertaking of the War on Poverty during the latter half of the 1960s bespoke the government's desire to have guns *and* butter at the same time. However, the refusal to pay for the Vietnam war effort through increased taxation ultimately sowed the seeds of an inflation problem that could not be solved by traditional means. At the same time, the programs designed to improve living standards for the poorest Americans were placing burdens on our productive capabilities that could not be satisfied.

SOCIAL SECURITY: FROM SAFETY NET TO ENTITLEMENT

The decade of the '60s would also bring momentous change to what had become a national institution—Social Security. Time would prove the change to be one in which the seeds of the program's potential destruction were planted. In 1937, the first full year of Social Security operation, 33 workers contributed to the benefits for each retiree. The maximum annual contribution of a working person, taxed at 1 percent of income, was only about $30, matched by a like amount from the employer.

Social Security was never intended as a primary pension program. Yet by the early 1970s Medicare had been grafted on and automatic cost-of-living increases had been built into the computation of benefits. Indeed, benefits had risen to the point where many persons began counting on them as their primary source of retirement income. It was at this point that Social Security ceased to be a "safety net" and became an inalienable right—an "entitlement."

PRESSURE COOKER: THE CRISIS BUILDS

By 1973, in a desperate attempt to quell the inflationary fires, the White House imposed wage and price controls on the economy. This was like tightening the lid of a pressure cooker. By 1975, the pressures had become so great that the lid blew off and this mechanism for controlling inflation was quickly abandoned.

The oil embargo of 1973 complicated matters even further. The Organization of Petroleum Exporting Countries (OPEC), exercising its monopolistic power over an oil-dependent world, raised petroleum prices sharply. This oil price shock was transmitted throughout the economies of the Free World, including the United States.

Contrary to popular belief, however, it was not the oil price increase itself that led to the spiraling inflation of the 1970s; rather, it was the Federal Reserve Board's response to that shock. Inflation is a monetary phenomenon; it reflects a situation where too much money is chasing too few goods.

What the Fed basically said was that if it did not allow the money supply to increase fast enough for Americans to buy not only the higher-priced energy-related commodities but everything else as well, the economy could be thrown into another depression. The Fed could only control the flow of money, not the supply of available goods and services. And its control over money supply was limited to the ability to manipulate a few key short-term interest rates. As a result, the Fed's policy of pumping money into the system transformed what would have been simply a cyclical pickup in inflation into a long-term upward spiral of the general price level.

Compounding an already serious problem was the fact that tax policy had completely neglected to provide incentives for saving and investing. In an attempt to redistribute income and fund ever more expensive government programs, tax rates were ratcheted up so the "rich" would pay their "fair share." By the end of the 1970s, high-income earners were facing a 70 percent top tax bracket on unearned income (interest and dividends) and a 50 percent maximum on wages and salaries.

Lawyers and accountants discovered loopholes in tax laws that had been adopted to foster certain valid economic activities. Using these loopholes, they devised clever tax shelters that enabled their clients to avoid the high tax rates—shelters that provided lucrative ways of investing in unproductive ventures that had little or no economic justification. By subverting the tax laws' meritorious motives, the process frustrated incentives to produce efficiently and provided disincentives to work. Savers, investors, and workers respond to what they earn after taxes. Taxes put a wedge between what we earn and what we keep. The bigger the tax wedge, the less desirable it becomes for us to put out work effort or to take risk. As a direct result of a high tax-rate structure, the growth potential of the United States was reduced.

A well-intentioned, though misguided, fiscal policy contributed to the instability of the economy during the 1970s. But in my opinion, the Federal Reserve Board must bear its share of the blame. The Fed believed the business cycle could be controlled by the careful manipulation of interest rates. The real target of the board's policy was long-term interest rates, but the only way it could influence the movement in long-term rates was through its control over short-term rates.

Here is how the maneuver worked. If the Fed wanted to lower long-term interest rates to stimulate the economy, it would lower the short-term rates that were directly under its control. Investors seeking to maintain high yields would then be able to do so only by buying bonds with longer maturities. The increased demand for these longer-maturity bonds would push up their prices. Because bond yields are inversely related to their prices, long-term interest rates would decline as the prices rose. Everybody was happy. The Fed lowered long rates, bond investors realized profits, and economic activity eventually responded as desired.

The problem in the 1970s was that this type of monetary manipulation, combined with fiscal stimulus, caused inflation to percolate through the system so that in each succeeding business cycle interest rates and inflation were both higher than they were in the preceding cycle. This process continued throughout the decade. Even when inflation and interest rates temporarily subsided, each cyclical low was higher than the previous one. That's the long of it. The short of it is that, simply put, the accelerating hyperinflation of the 1970s was caused by aggregate demand growing faster than the economy's ability to supply it.

BAD THINGS FROM GOOD INTENTIONS (CRISIS REDUX)

Real economic growth stagnated during the 1970s, productivity advances slowed to a crawl, inflation raged at a double-digit annual rate, and interest rates reached heights not seen before or since in American history. What kept making matters worse was that all of the policy tools that were being used were oriented in the wrong direction. This series of events gave rise to the term *stagflation*, a situation where sluggish economic growth and accelerating inflation were marching hand in hand. To restore price stability through demand-side policies at this point would have required dampening aggregate demand to depression levels, a policy option that would have been politically and rationally impossible.

As you would expect, this convergence of economic events and the misguided application of policies created a hostile environment for investors. Soaring interest rates depressed bond prices. At its peak in 1979, inflation was advancing at a 13 percent annual rate. If allowed to continue at that pace, it would cut purchasing power in half in just five and a half years. Because the tax laws prevented businesses from adequately accounting for inflation in their depreciation schedules, real corporate profits (operating earnings) collapsed. Investor confidence in the viability of the economic system and the government's ability to implement effective economic policies fell dramatically.

Once again, the stock market reflected the economic environment. The Dow Jones Industrial Average, which had reached a peak of 1052 in 1972, had lost about half its value by 1974. Over the subsequent five years, it recovered from this loss; by 1979 the Dow again reached 1000—the same level it had attained in 1966. In effect, the Dow went nowhere in 13 years. In real terms, however, when adjusted for inflation, the Dow had lost 80 percent of its value. Policies do indeed matter.

The decade of the '70s closed with expensive new government programs on the books and scheduled to grow rapidly, with tax revenues stagnating, and with existing economic policies apparently impotent to deal with the problems at hand. So it is that this chapter ends on a note close to the one on which it began. Just as economists and historians may disagree over the precise causes of the Great Depression, so may they disagree over the precise causes of the economic malaise that greeted the 1980s. But what seems clear now, as then, is that a conflux of unfortunate policy decisions had brought the U.S. economy to the brink. For the second time in 50 years, the economy appeared on the verge of collapse.

CHAPTER 3

THE 1980S:
RENAISSANCE OR RELAPSE?

"Every individual endeavors to employ his capital so that its produce be of greatest value. He generally neither intends to promote the public interest, nor knows how much he is promoting it. He intends only his own security, only his own gain. And he is in this led by an 'invisible hand' to promote an end that was no part of his intention. By pursuing his own interest he frequently promotes that of society more effectively than when he really intends to promote it."
—ADAM SMITH, *The Wealth of Nations*, 1776

THE BIRTH OF SUPPLY-SIDE ECONOMICS

By the late 1970s, a series of well-intentioned but misguided economic policies presented the American people with a crisis potentially as destructive to our way of life as the one the nation had faced in the 1930s. But it was an economic dilemma unlike any the country had ever seen. Our government, as it will from time to time, rose to the challenge. Policymakers summoned top economic experts to Washington to do two things: explain the nature of the new economic crisis and suggest what the government could do about it in order to save the economic system.

What government officials were told shocked them. All of our policy tools were oriented in the wrong direction, said the experts. The tools they were using were developed in the crucible of the depression to deal with the severe demand problems of the 1930s. But the problem they were facing in the 1970s was entirely different. The challenge was no longer one of demand but one of supply. The economy's ability to produce goods and services efficiently could no longer keep pace with the demands being put upon the system.

For traditional demand-side economic policies to be effective in reducing the inflationary fires raging in the U.S. economy, said the experts, the government would have to engineer a deep and prolonged recession. Politically and practically, this approach would be disastrous. However, there was an alternative. Rather than dampening demand, government policymakers could focus on developing economic policies that would unleash the productive potential of the American economy. This was the genesis of what later became known as *supply-side* economics.

It is commonly accepted that the new economic philosophy embodied a conservative Republican agenda that was forced upon the American people by a new administration and a conservative Congress. However, those signing the January 1980 Report of the Joint Economic Committee of Congress reveal the bipartisan support for the revolution in economic policy that was about to occur. This report stated clearly the nature of the policies that had to be developed in order to restore economic health to the United States. The policy prescriptions recommended by the Joint Economic Committee were later enacted into law nearly in their entirety. The signatories to this report up to that point had represented the loyal opposition to these market-oriented policies. Once again, economic realities were making strange bedfellows.

This new philosophy would represent a 180-degree change in direction from everything we had been doing since the Great Depression. While demand-management policies meant giving consumers and businesses incentives to spend, supply-side policies required the creation of incentives to save and invest. Only by increasing the savings and investment rate, it was reasoned, could the United States hope to increase its long-term potential growth rate.

The quickest and best way to expand the nation's productive capacity, the economic advisors told the government, was to cut taxes. "Great," said the politicians. "Everyone loves a tax cut."

"But you have to cut taxes in a certain way," the economists quickly added. "You have to persuade productive individuals to increase their work effort and build their savings. When the intent is to encourage people to save and invest, the bulk of any tax reduction should be given to the people who can be counted on to save and invest. These people are at the middle and upper end of the income range."

This was exactly the opposite of the prescription for the ills of the depression, when the objective was to give the greatest tax cuts to those we could count on to spend most of the tax reduction. These individuals were typically at the lower end of the income range.

Not surprisingly, the politicians balked. "Wait a minute," they said. "We can't get away with that because it isn't fair. These people are affluent and they don't need a tax cut."

The "F" word again. The politicians, of course, were speaking of fair as a synonym for economic justice. The government found itself between a rock and a hard place. If it was to prevent the demise of capitalism, the government would have to abandon efforts to foster economic justice through income and wealth redistribution. The economic advisors told the politicians, in effect, that to prevent the collapse of our economic system, economic efficiency must take precedence over economic justice. Economic policies would have to be oriented toward enhancing the desirability to save, invest, and produce, irrespective of the ultimate distribution of income and wealth that would be created.

The rationale for lowering tax rates was that the existing tax structure was providing disincentives to save, invest, and produce. The economic experts the government had summoned to Washington reasoned that by lowering tax rates in a dynamic economy the country could *increase* tax revenues over time.

LESS IS MORE: ENTER THE LAFFER CURVE

This supply-side philosophy was encapsulated in a sketch Professor Arthur Laffer, then a member of the faculty at the University of Southern California, made on the back of a napkin in a Los Angeles restaurant. The *Laffer Curve*, as it later became known, was used for descriptive purposes only. But its simplicity and its logic are difficult to refute (see Figure 3.1).

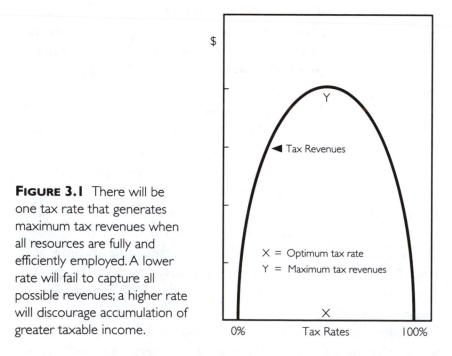

FIGURE 3.1 There will be one tax rate that generates maximum tax revenues when all resources are fully and efficiently employed. A lower rate will fail to capture all possible revenues; a higher rate will discourage accumulation of greater taxable income.

On the figure, the vertical axis represents tax revenues and the horizontal axis represents tax rates. It is clear that there are two tax rates that will generate no revenue. If the government imposes a tax rate of zero on all income, obviously no revenue will result. Similarly, if a 100 percent tax rate were levied on all income, no revenue would be generated, since no one would work. Logic tells us that there will be one rate somewhere between zero and 100 percent that will maximize revenue to the government when all available resources are fully and efficiently employed. This tax rate would be represented by X in the diagram and the revenues generated would be represented by Y.

Economists argued that the tax structure then in place provided disincentives to work. By reducing tax rates, they believed, after-tax income would rise, providing a powerful incentive to increase the work effort. If the tax rates on income, capital gains, and corporate profits were lowered, economic growth would be enhanced over the long term. Since lower tax rates would be levied on more income, tax receipts, over time, would also grow.

The debate over changes in the tax laws would rage for more than two years. When finally enacted, the legislation represented a change in economic philosophy no less profound than the one that had occurred during the Keynesian revolution of the 1930s. As we will see, the new law's economic and investment implications were just as far reaching.

MONETARY POLICY AT THE CROSSROADS: THE REINING IN OF THE FED

At the same time this debate on tax legislation was in its infancy, another phenomenon was taking place. Bond investors, who had been enticed time and again by the Federal Reserve Board into buying bonds, only to suffer erosion of their purchasing power and capital value by inflation, took control. Now more experienced and sophisticated, fixed-income investors began to watch Fed policy very carefully for any hint of an inflationary bias.

Should the board begin to push interest rates down prematurely—before the markets believed such a move was warranted by economic fundamentals—bond investors, given their experience with this type of policy in the past, would now sell their bonds in anticipation of the expected inflation. That would cause bond prices to fall and long-term interest rates to rise—exactly what the Fed was trying to avoid. In this way, investor anticipation became a binding constraint on Federal Reserve policy.

The credit markets literally took control of monetary policy. It became apparent, especially to the Fed, that if the board was to achieve its long-term objectives of price stability and economic growth, monetary policy would now have to *follow* the market, not lead it.

On October 6, 1979, Paul Volcker, then chairman of the Federal Reserve Board, acknowledged the market's control over monetary policy in a major announcement that most people did not believe. Basically, he said the Fed could no longer feasibly dictate the level of long-term interest rates in the United States. From here on, the chairman said, the market would dictate interest-rate levels. Only by allowing the free movement of the supply and demand for credit could we expect to see interest rates at levels necessary to foster noninflationary growth.

In essence, the Fed changed its focus from fixing interest rates to managing the money supply and credit flows in a noninflationary way over the long run. So was begun the era of the "bond market vigilantes." The bond market was now in control of monetary policy; interest rates would be determined by market forces, not the whims of the Federal Reserve Board.

The following example should not be interpreted as an attempt to give a rigorous and technical description of the intricacies of monetary policy. Rather, it provides a shorthand way of capturing the essence of the dilemma facing the Fed in the conduct of monetary policy. We can visualize this change in monetary policy by picturing a long stick. At each end of the stick is one objective of monetary policy; the money supply on one end, interest rates on the other. At any given time, the Fed can control one end of the stick or the other, but not both. Until 1979, the Fed had been concentrating on the interest-rate end, in effect, holding it steady at some predetermined level, allowing the money-supply end to rise or fall as fast or as slowly as necessary to maintain the interest rate target.

By 1979, that policy had generated so much inflation that the markets had grabbed control. Bond investors had learned to anticipate Fed efforts to manipulate long-term interest rates. By adjusting their investment plans accordingly, they were able to cancel out or reverse the Fed's desired intention. As a consequence, the Fed was forced to let go of the interest-rate end of the stick in order to grab the money-supply end. The board determined that it would let interest rates move wherever they needed to in order to achieve long-term price stability. The impact on the credit markets was immediate. Given the pressures that existed in the credit markets at that time, interest rates exploded upward. It was as if a balloon had been held at the bottom of a swimming pool and then let go.

The extent of the distortions built into the system became apparent as the prime rate, the rate at which banks lend to their best and most solid customers, soared to $21\frac{1}{2}$ percent. Interest rates on long-term Treasury bonds jumped to $15\frac{1}{4}$ percent. Money-market mutual funds were generating rates upwards of 18 percent. The Fed was now clearly following the dictates of the marketplace. If the markets determined that these interest-rate levels were appropriate for economic conditions, the Fed was willing to tolerate them. Should the market believe that lower interest rates were appropriate, the Fed was prepared to follow those interest rates down.

This new operating procedure was forced upon the monetary authorities. They had no choice but to yield to the power of the marketplace. If they wanted lower interest rates over the long run and they tried to push those rates down, they would end up with higher rates. The Fed was being constrained by the marketplace to pursue a policy that superseded political concerns and that over the long run would dampen the inflationary fires in the United States.

THE SELLING OF TAX REFORM: "EQUAL" CUTS FOR EVERYONE

Meanwhile, the debate over tax reform continued. During the discussions, many in the media and in Congress pointed out again and again that the kinds of tax changes being recommended to restore a more efficiently functioning economy would not treat people fairly. Affluent people don't need tax cuts, the critics said repeatedly. The response from tax-reduction proponents, in effect, was that the goal was economic efficiency, not economic justice. The salvation of the economic system would require bold new initiatives, they said, and a growing economy would benefit Americans in all income classes. A rising tide would raise all boats.

Congress was faced with no choice, however. In the end, it was forced to sell the concept to the American people by dissembling. The legislators did not lie; they simply disguised the truth. They were able to persuade their constituents that spreading the reduction in marginal tax rates over a three-year period was "fair" and that regardless of their individual income levels, all Americans would experience the same reductions in their marginal tax brackets (10 percent in 1982, 10 percent in 1983, and 5 percent in 1984). What could be more fair than that?

To understand the real intent of the government in recommending this form of tax reduction, you have to turn the proposal upside down and look at what it would do to after-tax income. Every accountant knows that the higher your income (and thus the higher your tax bracket) the bigger the increase in your after-tax income will be from a given reduction in the marginal tax rate. As written, and ultimately enacted, the bulk of the tax cut would accrue to higher-income individuals—the savers and the investors.

It is important to note that in its pursuit of this goal, the government was confronted with a make-or-break situation. It had no other workable alternative. As I noted earlier, this philosophical change was bipartisan in nature and, while history may not record it thus, it was one of our government's finest hours. The new economic philosophy culminated in the tax act of 1981 when the major portion of the largest tax cut in U.S. history was granted to high-income individuals and corporations—not to make the rich richer, as many have claimed, but to avert an economic crisis of potentially mammoth proportions.

Besides reducing income taxes for the middle and upper income groups, the 1981 tax act cut corporate and capital gains taxes, provided investment tax credits, accelerated depreciation allowances, and liberalized individual retirement accounts as other effective ways to increase the amount of savings and investment in the United States. Growth became the primary objective of economic policy; economic justice was only a secondary concern. The tax act of 1981 represented a major change in economic philosophy unlike anything since the Keynesian revolution of the 1930s. This sea change in policy was greeted by many Americans with confusion and apprehension.

THE BUDGET DEFICIT: FACT AND FICTION

Complicating matters further, the United States would soon embark upon a massive buildup of its national defense. While not apparent at the time, the country was about to challenge the Soviet Union to a competition the Soviets could not win. Our secret weapon: our economic system. There was wide-spread concern that tax reduction and the speedup of govern-ment spending would lead to growing budget deficits and that our national debt, which at the beginning of the 1980s was around $1 trillion, could triple over the ensuing 10 years.

Since before the end of World War II, the planet's two largest powers had stood toe to toe, maintaining a tenuous neutrality in a war of nerves and ever-escalating weapons development. Neither side could win the Cold War militarily without con-suming the earth in a nuclear holocaust, and neither side could win the hearts and minds of the other's people because of dia-metrically opposed views of liberty and human rights. In the end, it was America's superior economic potential that carried the day. The strategic defense initiative, the sophisticated (and highly expensive) weapons-development program that became known as Star Wars, was the ultimate vehicle.

We gave the Soviets this message: "We are going to build a strong defense system and you will be forced to match our strength. We may have to commit 7 percent of our economy to achieve our end, but you will have to devote 50 percent of yours. You will not be able to compete."

Thus did the United States, a marathon runner, challenge the Soviet Union, a sprinter, to an endurance race. After the first hundred yards, we knew they would be way ahead of us. Maybe after the first mile or five miles, they would still be ahead. But by mile 15 or 20, we would be firmly and lastingly in the lead.

The Soviets realized the inevitability of the outcome, but there was little they could do about it. This economic strategy did not come without considerable cost; between 1980 and 1990, America added $2 trillion to its national debt, tripling its total indebtedness. In a sense, though, that extra $2 trillion can be viewed not as a consumption expense, but a capital expenditure. In other words, the investment would pay lasting dividends to our posterity somewhere down the line. It was, in effect, the cost of breaking up the Soviet Union.

At this point, it is necessary to try to put the national debt and the federal budget deficit into perspective. It is a topic much discussed and much misunderstood. Is the deficit really a problem? There are a couple of ways to look at it. One, we have to consider who owns the national debt. The impression often given these days is that the Japanese own most of it. The fact is, however, that 83 percent of our country's total debt outstanding is owned by Americans.

Think for a moment. Would you like to have twice as many U.S. Series E savings bonds or U.S. Treasury notes in your safe-deposit box tomorrow as you have today? Most of us would answer yes, of course. We regard them as secure storehouses of value, and they earn interest. The more of them we have, the better we feel. Americans treat these bonds as assets, not liabilities, on their personal balance sheets.

But what about the interest on the national debt? It represents a major cost item in the federal budget. So it does; however, 83 percent of this interest goes to the Americans who own the securities. And that interest is treated as income on which the holders of these securities pay taxes, providing revenue for the government and thus partially offsetting the cost of maintaining the debt. Maybe we should consider the outstanding liability of the federal government as a national asset, not a national debt. After all, we owe most of the money to ourselves.

Furthermore, the dollar size of the national debt is not important. Now, I know this is a controversial statement, but it is true and it represents a concept that is necessary to understand in order to put the debt situation into proper perspective. It does not matter to the health of our economy whether we have a $1 trillion debt as we did in 1980 or a $3 trillion debt as it stood by the end of the decade. What is important is that the government adopt economic policies over time that allow our economy to grow faster than the debt is accumulating. That is the trick.

As an example of how confusion between the absolute size of our debt and the relative size of our debt can cause undue anxiety, let's look back at the situation just after World War II. The United States was poised for a long period of growth and prosperity. At that time, one year's gross domestic product (GDP), the total value of all goods and services produced in the country in one year, was around $100 billion. Yet the country's total national debt in 1946 was about $120 billion—120 percent of a year's GDP. And this debt did not prevent the long period of prosperity that followed the war because the economy was growing faster than the debt was accumulating. This resulted in a continuous decline in the outstanding debt relative to the size of the economy.

Today, our nation's debt is $4.9 trillion. That's 2000 percent higher than it was in 1946. But our GDP is more than $7 trillion; now our government owes only 70 percent of a year's GDP. I don't know about you, but I know I would feel better about my financial future if I owed 70 percent of a year's income than if I owed 120 percent. The important thing is to keep this ratio on a declining path.

There is a right way and a wrong way to deal with our debt. The wrong way is to deal with it directly by cutting expenditures and raising taxes. In the long run, this will depress the economy and may actually worsen the debt situation. The correct way to deal with the deficit is indirectly, through growth. If government expenditures can be constrained to grow more slowly than the economy, and growth-oriented tax policy enables revenues to grow in line with the economy, the deficit will diminish over time. These numbers, reflecting our debt, are of Brobdingnagian proportions and almost impossible to comprehend. For example, if we were to count one dollar per second, it would take us 95,129 years to count to three trillion. Thank goodness these numbers are meaningless.

ENTITLEMENTS: THE TIME BOMB KEEPS TICKING

While the policymakers were busy shaping the new economic environment, demographic trends, which had been moving glacially for decades, were beginning to have an impact. Over the years, through a combination of increased life expectancy, fewer workers entering the workforce, and more retirees drawing benefits from the Social Security system, the ratio of workers to retirees had steadily declined. By 1960, 15 workers supported each retiree. As the 1980s began, this ratio had shrunk to four to one. To meet the large and growing burden of providing ever-increasing Social Security and Medicare benefits, tax rates to finance these programs were continually increased. From the modest 2 percent combined rate paid by employees and employers on the first $3,000 of income to support Social Security payments in 1937, the combined levy stood at 12.26 percent on the first $25,900 of income by the beginning of the 1980s.

Meanwhile, the baby-boomer population bulge continued its march through life's stages toward retirement. Clearly, demographic trends were moving in a direction that was beginning to threaten the long-term solvency of the Social Security system. So, in 1981, the government quietly took the first step toward defusing the ticking bomb. Acknowledging the increasing longevity of Americans, Congress passed legislation that would require all Americans who were 23 years of age or younger in 1981 to be 67 years old before they would be eligible for maximum Social Security benefits, up from 65. To make this change palatable and to give the baby boomers a way of generating a supplemental pool of capital on which to earn income when they retire, Congress made the individual retirement account (IRA) universally available.

THE GAMBLE PAYS OFF

The quote from Adam Smith in *The Wealth of Nations* that opens this chapter captures the laissez-faire philosophy of the 1980s. Smith stated, in essence, that every individual seeks the greatest personal gain from capital, without regard to the public interest. Even so, these individual efforts, led by an "invisible hand," generally unintentionally promote the public good, and often these unintended benefits to society are more effective than efforts deliberately taken to promote the public welfare. Cynical observers of the economic scene have labeled this economic truth *trickle-down* economics. Yet, like it or not, this is the way our system works.

R. Buckminster Fuller, the architect-inventor-author, used the analogy of honeybees to illustrate the presence of unintended benefits. Bees, he said, are driven to gather nectar so they can make honey to sustain themselves. But, in that process, they also pollinate flowers, an act essential to the propagation of the flowers.

The principle can be demonstrated in an economic setting, as well. When policies are undertaken to produce growth in the economy as a whole, a valuable by-product is that over time we all tend to become better off individually. As discussed earlier, however, this process does not mean "equally" better off. Because the economic policies pursued during the 1980s were appropriate for dealing with the problems at hand, the nation experienced the longest economic expansion since World War II. In eight and a half years, the annual inflation rate dropped from more than 13 percent to 1 percent. Interest rates on long-term Treasury bonds declined by more than half, from 15 percent to 7 percent. Employment soared, with 22 million more workers employed within a seven-year period, taking the employment rate to historically high levels. The decade of "greed" was not without its benefits.

Concerns over huge budget deficits and the fear of economic collapse, which had kept many investors on the sidelines in the early stages of this debate, gradually gave way to growing optimism about economic prospects. Investors who saw clearly this revolution in economic thought were able to position their assets to take full advantage of the approaching stock market tidal wave. Many investors, however, took a full year after the tax legislation was signed into law to digest what was happening. When they did, the financial markets celebrated the economic renaissance by exploding. The Dow Jones Industrial Average, which by August 12, 1982, had dropped to 777, nearly one-third below its peak in 1966, jumped 236 points within a 60-day period between August 12 and October 11, an increase of 30 percent. So began the bull market of the 1980s that would result in more than a threefold rise between 1982 and the end of the decade.

THE PENDULUM SWINGS BACK

As the economy again started growing and becoming more efficient, the invisible hand of the marketplace was at work. While most Americans were enjoying the renewed economic prosperity, all were not benefiting at the same rate. A widespread and not entirely erroneous impression was that the rich were growing richer and the poor were becoming poorer. In fact, the more productive were getting ahead faster than the less productive, the predictable outcome of a free-market philosophy. As the decade unfolded, the income distribution had become more skewed as the wealth of the nation accrued more and more to those who were producing it, and in proportion to their contribution. Despite the statistically indisputable fact of increasing prosperity, dissatisfaction grew.

The desire to rectify this cruel result of market-oriented policies led to a predictable reaction. The American people

shifted their attention away from the economic consequences
of these policy actions. Economic justice once again took center
stage. The economic system was seen as growing increasingly
unfair. In addition, the budget deficit was seen as a clear and
present danger to our way of life, and a monstrous threat to future generations.

Even though the debt was being reduced as a proportion of
the total economy, the government adopted a direct approach to
dealing with the deficit. Tax increases were relied upon to close
the widening budget gap. Furthermore, in an attempt to correct
the growing imbalances between income groups, tax increases
were to fall on those who were able to afford them. The "rich"
would pay their "fair share." Tax rates were raised on high-
income individuals, as were taxes on corporations. Government
spending restraint was also introduced.

Thus, in 1990, the economic philosophy that so dominated
the 1980s was slowly being dismantled. This change in policy
direction ended the longest economic expansion since World
War II and plunged the U.S. economy into a recession that
spanned 1990 and 1991. Despite efforts to rein in the budget
deficit—in my opinion, *because* of these efforts—the deficits
grew worse. It was like a tiger chasing its own tail. As the economy receded and unemployment grew, higher tax rates were
levied on less income, and revenues fell short of expectations.

The American people became fixated on the budget deficit
and perceived an inherent unfairness in the philosophy of supply-side policies. The result was that by 1992 the American
people abandoned this economic philosophy and elected a new
government whose primary challenge was to slay the budget
dragon once and for all and make the distribution of income
and wealth in the United States more equitable. The battle cry
became, "Those who made it in the '80s would pay for it in the
'90s." The implication was that if you responded to incentives
to work, save, and invest, you were somehow acting immorally.
The "decade of greed" was about to end.

The tax act of 1993 effectively dismantled the remnants of the supply-side philosophy. Marginal tax rates on income and capital gains were increased dramatically for high-income earners, and corporate tax rates were raised again. Once more the pendulum was swinging, but this time in a direction that would emphasize economic justice at the expense of economic efficiency. As we will see, this philosophical shift had within it the seeds of its own destruction and perhaps has set the stage for an era of economic growth and prosperity not witnessed since the early 1980s. Those who are prepared and act appropriately will be able to set a course for financial independence.

CHAPTER 4

THE DAWNING OF THE
NEW ECONOMIC ERA

"In a time of exploding change—with personal lives being torn apart, the existing social order crumbling, and a fantastic new way of life emerging on the horizon—asking the very largest of questions about our future is not merely a matter of intellectual curiosity. It is a matter of survival."
—ALVIN TOFFLER, *The Third Wave*, 1980

THE NEXT WAVE: THE NEW PHILOSOPHY

Major events are among the most important sculptors of economic and investment history. Like so many other things in life, these events are unpredictable. When they occur, however, they almost always carry profound implications for investors—both positive and negative. Protectionism in the 1930s, the Great Depression, and the Keynesian revolution are representative of the major events that shaped the course of economic and investment history in this century. As we saw in the preceding chapter, so, too, was the crisis of the late 1970s and the supply-side revolution that sprang from it. Even more recently and with its implications still unfolding, we experienced another major economic event in November 1994—the election that reversed the balance of power in Congress for the first time in 40 years.

Investors who recognize these watershed events and act early and appropriately are often able to position their assets for maximum advantage. So far, the mass media and financial press have missed the significance of the 1994 election for investors. They speak about that election in terms of its political and social implications. Some gloat that it was a Republican victory, others lament that it was a Democratic defeat. A few see it as the harbinger of a change in presidential administrations. What that election really represents, however, is a major shift in economic philosophy as profound as the change that occurred in the early 1980s, and the implications for investors are as far-reaching.

Americans must recognize the election's real but still obscured importance as the catalyst needed to start planning for their financial future. Much will be written about what is to unfold in Washington and the major dramatic changes that are to take place on the economic policy landscape. It is important for all of us to maintain our objectivity and to cut through what will undoubtedly be volumes of political rhetoric.

If there is a lesson to be drawn from what we have already discussed, it is this: when economic policies are oriented in a direction that will enhance economic growth, moderate inflation and interest rates, provide employment opportunities for workers to realize their full economic potential, and promote greater corporate profitability, the economic environment will become highly conducive to equity investing and the accumulation of wealth. We must, however, steel ourselves to the inevitable implications for economic justice.

Have no illusions. This coming change in the focus of policy will make life more difficult for some Americans. That was also true in the 1980s. But the government is being forced to abandon its attempts to pursue its desire for economic justice. The consequences of not doing so would threaten the viability of our economic system to the detriment of all. As we have seen, achieving economic objectives may preclude the attainment of some of our social goals. While this may be disheartening to you and seem unfair, you must not take your eye off the ball. Investment decisions must be based upon economic realities and the investment consequences of government action.

We are about to witness a serious discourse on tax reform and spending restraint. This dialogue will be reminiscent of the one that began in 1979 and culminated in the tax act of 1981. It will again be bipartisan in nature. The reason for this new debate over major changes in the way our government manages our economic affairs is that policymakers are once more facing a situation in which they have no choice if they are to save our economic system. What is becoming apparent to them is that if the economic expansion that started in 1991 were to stall, our government would be powerless to do anything about it by traditional means.

Think of our economic system as a 100-car freight train being pulled by an engine. The engine breaks down, but instead of repairing it, the crew proceeds to adjust the brakes on the caboose and check the couplings between the freight cars. While these are essential tasks to ensure a safe trip, the plain fact is that until the crew works on the stalled engine, that train is not going anywhere. In a figurative sense, Washington's legislators and economic policymakers have been working on the caboose and the freight cars. At last, economic circumstances are forcing our government to focus on the engine.

The Problem

If you will recall, during the 1930s, monetary policy had become impotent to deal with the business cycle. Interest rates could not be pushed low enough to entice people and businesses to borrow and spend. The condition was defined as a liquidity trap. Now, once again, this situation seems to exist. To illustrate, in 1990, the federal funds rate, a rate directly controlled by the Federal Reserve Board, peaked at $9\frac{1}{2}$ percent. The Fed ultimately reduced that rate to 3 percent, bringing the real rate (the difference between the market rate and inflation) virtually to zero before the economy started to recover.

Nearly four years later, at the peak of the business cycle in 1994, the federal funds rate had apparently topped out at 6 percent. From this level, the Federal Reserve Board does not have much room for maneuvering and, as Chairman Alan Greenspan reminded us when the Fed trimmed rates slightly in the summer of 1995, interest rates cannot drop below zero. It appears that monetary policy has once again lost its ability to stimulate economic activity.

Further mirroring events in the 1930s, this situation is not confined solely to the United States. In Japan, the discount rate (the rate at which the central bank lends money to financial institutions) stands at one-half of 1 percent. The Group of 7 (G-7, the leading industrialized democracies that meet from time to time to discuss international economic and related issues)* is urging the Japanese to stimulate their economy by fiscal means—the Keynesian prescription.

While fiscal stimulation was an option for the United States in the 1930s, it is no longer an option today. To use Keynesian remedies today to stimulate economic activity would require large increases in government spending and sharp reductions in taxes. Furthermore, we would start this process with a budget deficit of about $165 billion, or approximately 2.3 percent of the U.S. gross domestic product. To restart a $7 trillion economy effectively might require a budget deficit of $700 billion, or 10 percent of GDP, which would be politically out of the question.

---

*Canada, France, Germany, Italy, Japan, United Kingdom, United States.

As a consequence of the tax act of 1993 and the well-intentioned attempt to foster economic justice, we now face a seemingly intractable problem. Simply stated, our tax system now seems incapable of generating enough revenue to meet expenditures, even if our economy were operating with all of our factories and resources fully employed. While this situation has not yet been carefully explained to the American people, it is the driving force behind this new change in economic philosophy.

We can use the Laffer Curve to illustrate the problem (Figure 4.1). We now know from historical experience that when the maximum tax rate was lowered in the 1980s from 70 percent to 28 percent, tax revenues grew throughout the decade, since these lower tax rates were levied on more income as the

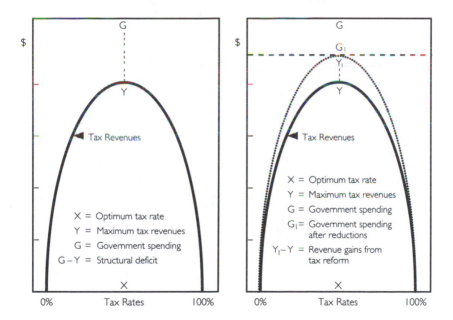

Figure 4.1 Even at optimum levels, as illustrated by the Laffer Curve, the current tax structure (left graph) is unable to provide sufficient revenues to eliminate the budget deficit, creating a "structural" deficit. Tax reforms may provide higher revenues (right graph), but only by also slowing the pace of spending growth can the budget's structural deficit be eliminated over time.

economy expanded. The problem we face today, however, is that even if the economy were operating at full employment, our current tax system could not generate enough tax revenues to meet government expenditures, represented by line G in Figure 4.1. The gap between the maximum amount of revenue the economy is capable of generating and the level of government spending is called a *structural deficit*. It is endemic to our system; we cannot grow out of it.

What is worse, beginning in 1997, economists estimate that if we do nothing, this structural deficit will again begin to grow. Not only will it be growing in dollar terms, which, as I have explained, is not necessarily important, it will be growing relative to the size of our economy. Should that trend develop, it could ultimately have a crushing impact on the economy, with devastating effects upon our way of life.

Since 1990, attempts to deal with the deficit have been direct in nature by focusing on cutting spending or raising taxes. Should this approach be taken now, however, it would require either draconian cuts in spending that would be politically impossible to achieve or tax increases that would depress economic activity and result in even less revenues and bigger budget deficits. Fortunately, our government has another option—improving the way the tax system functions; in effect, making it more efficient. This can be depicted in the diagram of the Laffer Curve (Figure 4.1) by raising the revenue curve (indicated by the broken line) so more revenue is generated at full employment. When combined with modest spending restraint, this combination could put the structural deficit on a declining path.

Tax Reform: The Dialogue Begins

With regard to tax reform, the debate that is now unfolding will deal with developing a tax system that would initially raise the same amount of revenue as the existing system but would be far more conducive to fostering economic growth over the long run. The direct benefit would be to put more people to work, which would add more revenue to the treasury from a growing tax base. Combined with meaningful spending restraint, this *indirect* approach to the deficit problem could lead to faster economic growth, higher levels of employment, improved standards of living, and diminishing budget deficits over time.

If we are going to make major changes in our tax system that will again encourage saving, investment, and improvements in productivity, and if we are to avoid exacerbating an already high federal budget deficit, we must find new and perhaps unorthodox ways to generate more tax revenue. As with any negotiation, at the outset of the debate on tax reform, we should expect to see proposals for increasing the efficiency of our tax system that represent extreme points of view. Not only is this starting point virtually inevitable, it is necessary in order to establish the boundaries of the debate. That done, the search can begin for the common ground that lies somewhere between the extremes.

Here are some of the concepts most likely to find their way onto the tax-reform agenda.

Income Tax

The general themes of proposals for changes in the current income tax system will be efficiency and simplification. One extreme might be characterized by the proposal of Republican Representative Dick Armey of Texas. Armey's version would eliminate all tax deductions, exempt from taxes interest and dividends from all sources, and ultimately have a single tax rate of 17 percent on all income. The appeal of a so-called flat tax lies in its simplicity and seeming fairness. One rate for all Americans, regardless of their income. What could be more *fair* than that? Does this sound familiar?

At the other extreme of the flat-tax discussion, Representative Richard Gephardt of Missouri, who represents the more liberal Democratic approach to economic policy matters, has recommended a five-tax rate system with a maximum rate of 34 percent. Still other variations of the flat-tax proposal would carry higher tax rates but allow some deductions. It would appear that Congress is setting up the parameters for a compromise that might entail an income tax system with more than one rate but fewer than five and with a maximum rate somewhere between 17 percent and 34 percent.

In the dialogue that is now unfolding, a substantial reduction in the capital gains tax rate is sure to be recommended. Experience has shown that lower capital-gains tax rates encourage risk-taking and free up capital to be employed in more productive ways. While it may be argued that this variant of tax reform is a sop to the "rich," the economic reality is that, in order to stimulate growth, we must enable capital to move freely and to its most productive use. Current capital-gains tax rates are an impediment to the efficient use of capital resources. Lowering the tax rate on capital gains has been a powerful incentive in the past for investors to unlock their capital and redeploy it in more productive enterprises.

Don't be surprised to see Congress follow up on the 1992 recommendation by the Treasury Department to end the double taxation of corporate dividends. The United States is the only country in the world that taxes dividends twice—once when the corporation earns its profits and pays taxes on them at the corporate rate, and again when the profits are paid out as dividends and the company's shareholders pay taxes on them at their individual rates. As a result of this double taxation, dividends face an effective tax rate upwards of 60 percent.

Consumption Tax

Forms of taxation other than a tax on income will also be included in this emerging dialogue. Since the late 1970s, economists have explored the feasibility of using a consumption-based tax in the United States. One proposal that has been offered by Senators Sam Nunn of Georgia and Pete Domenici of New Mexico has found support from Representative Bill Archer of Texas, head of the House Ways and Means Committee. This proposal would eliminate the income tax system altogether. These legislators ask the question: "Why tax people on what they put *into* the economy?" Let them keep all of their income. Tax people only on what they take *out* of the system.

Here is how such a consumption tax would work. You would sum up your income from all sources during the year. From this total, you would subtract all of the money you put into savings and investments during the year (CDs, stocks, mutual funds, and so on), as well as any extraordinary medical expenditures. By definition, what remained would represent what you had consumed during the year. That would be the tax base upon which the government would levy taxes at a progressive rate, ranging from 14 percent to a maximum rate of 40 percent. To reduce your taxes, all you would have to do is increase the amount of your income that you save or invest. Talk about extremes. Can you see the intent of this proposal?

PAYING FOR TAX REFORM

If we are going to make major changes in our tax system that would again encourage saving, investment, and improved productivity, and if we are to avoid worsening our budget deficit, we must find new and perhaps innovative ways of generating revenue in the United States. As I have said, economists have been exploring the feasibility of using consumption taxes since the 1970s. Two that will be part of the dialogue are described next.

National Sales Tax

While sales taxes, a variant of consumption taxes, have long been a popular means by which states and localities have generated revenues, a sales tax at the federal level seems to offend the American sense of fairness.

The argument has been and will continue to be that the burden of these consumption taxes falls on those least able to pay it. Those individuals who consume most or all of their income, it is argued, would pay a proportionately higher share of this tax. A way around the argument that is sure to be recommended would be to exempt from a national sales tax those items that loom large in a low-income budget—food, medicine, shelter, heat, utilities, and the like. Given the economic realities now facing our government, the American people should prepare themselves for a major debate on this issue.

Value-added Tax

A form of sales tax popular in many European countries, a value-added tax (VAT) is levied on the value added to a product at each stage of its production. The taxes added along the way are ultimately reflected in the final price of the product. By way of example, a 3 percent value-added tax in the United States would generate about $120 billion a year in new revenue to the government, after excluding such personal essentials as just noted and capital equipment for businesses.

Another argument offered in favor of some form of consumption tax is that it would capture revenue missed by an income tax. Some estimates claim that the unreported—and thus untaxed—income represented by the underground economy in the United States exceeds $1 trillion a year. It has just dawned on our government that no matter how high income tax rates are raised, you cannot generate revenue from income that is not reported, and the higher the tax rates, the greater the temptation to find ways to "hide" income from taxation.

The attraction of a consumption tax is that the government gets the revenue when the income is *spent*, not when it is earned. That could represent an additional $30 billion a year in taxes that would drop right out of the sky from income that is not now reported. These revenues generated from such taxes could be used to pay for the tax reduction on savings, investments, and income.

I have made no attempt here to provide a comprehensive list of tax-reform proposals that will find their way into the debate, because the variety of possible offerings is infinite and is certain to include some that defy the imagination. I am mentioning these various schemes only because they will become part of the ongoing dialogue that will monopolize the financial headlines for the next several years. My intent here is not to make a case for any particular tax or spending scheme, but rather to highlight examples of proposals that you should take very seriously when assessing the economic and investment climate that will be unfolding. Don't make the mistake that so many made in the 1980s and write off this debate as so much political hogwash. That could be hazardous to your financial well-being.

I will offer this one suggestion as you follow the debate. Watch for new terms to be introduced into the lexicon of tax reform. You will hear tax-reform proposals recommended as being *revenue neutral*. When you hear this term mentioned, a little bell should sound in your head. It will be a clue to the ultimate intent of government policy. Revenue neutrality means nothing more than raising taxes in one area while reducing them in others. The effect on the flow of tax revenue initially would be zero, or neutral. The initial effect on our budget deficit would be zero, or neutral. But the growth that could be unleashed by such tax reforms could allow tax revenues over time to grow in line with our economy, just as they did during the 1980s.

Government Spending: From Entitlement to Safety Net

While an overhaul of our tax structure should enable the government to construct a more efficient tax system, that represents just half of the challenge. The other half will entail reversing 50 years of social policy. I realize that what I am about to discuss will be upsetting to many, but I must remind you again that this book is not about what we wish would happen, or what we hope will happen, but about the economic facts of life and how to profit from them. And the most pressing fact of life for most of us in this new economic era is that the government will not be able to continue handing out benefits with the same largesse that we have come to expect.

Increasingly, the government will be asking those of us who are able to provide for ourselves to do so to a greater extent than we might have anticipated until now. It will, however, provide ways to help those of us who are still young to start taking greater responsibility for our financial future. It will be asking those who are closer to retirement to rethink the concept of retirement at age 65. It will be telling those who are already retired not to expect to see benefits rise each year as generously as they have in the past.

The good news is that the government will not leave us stranded. It will not take something away without providing something else to hang onto. For example, do not be surprised to hear discussions about various new government-sponsored programs that will allow Americans to provide for their own retirement needs. Expanded individual retirement account (IRA) programs, which will again allow all Americans to participate and which may provide more generous annual tax-deferral limits than at present, will be introduced, along with other programs.

The government is about to let the American people in on a dirty little secret: the economy can no longer support the continued growth of many of the social programs instituted over the past 50 years. While politicians are reluctant to articulate this message in so many words, the handwriting is clearly on the wall. Successfully achieving financial security requires that each of us recognizes these emerging trends and takes the appropriate action now.

We have seen how Social Security and Medicare programs have evolved from safety nets to entitlement programs. When we consider that, on average, according to the Social Security Administration, 38 percent of retirement income for persons over 65 is derived from Social Security payments, and for many retirees it represents the bulk of their retirement income, it becomes clear that many individuals view Social Security as a pension plan. Economic reality is now forcing the government to unravel this web of benefits it has promised to individuals now and in the future—benefits most of us, as actual or potential recipients, have come to regard as inalienable rights: Social Security, Medicare, Medicaid, and welfare payments of various types. There is one major problem with these entitlements, well-meaning and politically attractive as they may be: there will not be enough money to pay for them.

This is an emotion-charged subject, and I know you probably have some strong views of your own about it. As I have said several times already, this book is not about the pros or cons of these benefits. It is not about whether these benefits are deserved or not, or about who should or should not receive them. Besides explaining how we got to where we are, this book's purpose is to tell you in the most emphatic terms that you should not be factoring these "paper" benefits into your financial future, because there is a virtual certainty that they will not be as generous as they are now and a better than even chance that many of them will not be available at all. The good news, though, is that if you act now, there are ways you can provide more than adequately for a secure financial future—on your own.

SOCIAL SECURITY: ALREADY ON THE ROPES

To make my case, here is some arithmetic about Social Security that you should bear in mind. Over the years, through a combination of increasing life expectancy, fewer workers entering the workforce, and more retirees drawing benefits from the system, the ratio of workers to retirees has steadily shrunk. By 1960, 15 workers supported each retiree. The ratio in the mid-1990s is about three and a half to one, and government estimates project that by the year 2029 each retiree will be supported by taxes from only two and a half workers.

Medicare, as an extension of Social Security, was designed to assure that all eligible Americans, regardless of their personal resources, would have hospital care in their old age. Medicaid, on the other hand, was designed to provide medical care for Americans of any age who could not afford it. Thus, it was truly an antipoverty program and was attached to the welfare system. Medicaid is financed and administered by participating states, with matching federal funds.

Like so many other government programs undertaken in the name of social and economic justice, Medicare and Medicaid were idealistic and well-intentioned efforts to help those who had difficulty helping themselves. In the legislative zeal to enact the programs, however, insufficient attention was paid to the fiscal time-bomb built into them.

To meet the large and growing burden of providing Social Security and Medicare benefits to all who are eligible to receive them, tax rates have had to increase dramatically. From 1937 to 1995, the tax rate has been progressively raised from 1 percent to 7.65 percent and the wage base on which the tax is levied has been increased from $3,000 to $61,200. The maximum annual contribution has therefore been increased from $30 a year to $4,682 a year and is matched by employer contributions. For many Americans, the Social Security tax has become the largest tax they pay. In 2029, when the Social Security trust fund is expected to be exhausted, a tax of 20 percent on every worker's entire income will be required to provide benefits for retired baby boomers at today's eligibility levels.

This amounts to a $7 trillion unfunded liability today. That is how much all benefits promised to today's participants exceed the scheduled payroll taxes and the $400 billion in assets now ascribed to the trust fund. I say "ascribed to," because the trust fund itself does not represent actual dollars on deposit somewhere. It is the accumulated total of IOUs the Treasury has written against the trust fund to meet current federal budget obligations. Thanks to the Employee Retirement Income Security Act of 1974 (ERISA), no private pension fund is legally allowed to work that way. To place the size of the liability in context, it is roughly equal to the current U.S. gross domestic product—the sum of the country's entire output of goods and services for a year.

Incomprehensible as that sum appears, the story gets worse. The unfunded liability of the health care system and the federal government's own pension system represents another $14 trillion—double a year's GDP. As we will see, this situation is untenable, and some very drastic measures will have to be taken immediately to save the Social Security/Medicare system.

When Social Security was instituted, a person retiring at age 65 had a seven-year life expectancy. Today, a person at that age is expected to live a full 16 years after retirement. The odds that a person aged 65 today will actually live to age 85 are much higher than they have ever been. (See Table 4.1. and Figure 4.2.) Don't be surprised to see the minimum age at which

TABLE 4.1 Life Expectancy: We Are Living Longer Now

Age	1940		1965		1990	
	Men	Women	Men	Women	Men	Women
65	12.1	13.6	12.9	16.2	15.1	18.9
70	9.5	10.6	10.4	12.8	12.0	15.3
75	7.2	8.0	8.1	9.7	9.4	12.0
80	5.4	6.0	6.2	7.0	7.1	9.0
85	4.1	4.5	4.5	4.8	5.2	6.4

Figures in table show life expectancy at various ages.
(Source: National Center for Health Statistics)

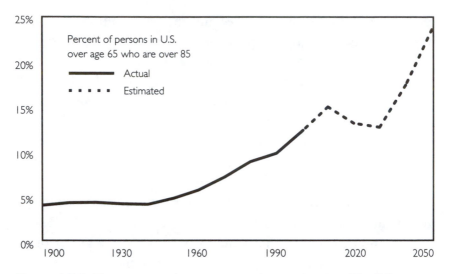

FIGURE 4.2 The prospect that someone who reaches age 65 will live to 85 and beyond has risen dramatically since the 1960s. Projections suggest the trend will continue into the 21st century. (Source: U.S. Bureau of the Census)

Americans can receive maximum Social Security benefits pushed even higher in the years to come, continuing the precedent set in 1981 when the age was raised to 67 for younger participants. The Commission on Entitlement and Tax Reform cochaired by Senator Bob Kerrey of Nebraska has recommended that the age be raised to 70. Make no mistake about it, the objective of our government is ultimately to push the baby boomers out to their actuarial limits, where many will die off before they receive the benefits to which they feel entitled.

Means testing for Social Security and Medicare will also be proposed; if your income is above a certain level when you retire, forget about taxing those benefits as is the case today— you will not get them at all. "Wait a minute," you might say. "Politicians wouldn't dare touch Social Security." Obviously, a politician would not go to the American Association of Retired Persons (AARP) or to a 55- or 60-year-old and ask for their votes on such a measure. However, they could very well ap-

proach a 21- or 30- or even a 40-year-old taxpayer with a convincing story. You see, there is no guesswork. We know who is
alive today and we know how many people will be working in
30 or 35 years. These demographic trends will capture the attention of these age groups, and that is where most of the
votes are.

And the demographics are indisputable. The question to be
put to the millions of Americans now working is this: "Would
you like to take the chance that you will get Social Security
and Medicare benefits at levels equivalent to today's when you
retire in 30 or 35 years, when that working population would
have to vote to tax themselves up to 20 percent of their income
to give it to you? Or would you rather have the ability now to
utilize an expanded and enhanced individual retirement account or some other tax-favored means to build a supplemental
pool of capital upon which to earn income when you retire or
to leave to your heirs?"

There is no doubt in my mind that the great majority of us
would prefer the latter—and more desirable—option. The
politicians know this, too. Only the voters can decide how
much they are willing to pay for someone else's retirement today against an uncertain political promise of what they themselves may receive in years to come. The unspoken message in
this new dialogue about the future of Social Security and
Medicare, especially to people under 40, is that you are now on
your own in determining your financial future. We all had better take this to heart, because whether we retire in 20 or 30 or
35 years, if we have not taken our financial destiny into our
own hands, the response from the government will be, "Tough.
We gave you ample opportunity to set something aside. You
knew what was coming."

Demographic, economic, and political realities being what
they are, it is a virtual certainty that, within the next decade,
Social Security and Medicare will cease being benefits to which
all of us are entitled and will revert to their original purpose—

to serve as safety nets for the neediest among us. Those who ignore this reality do so at their own peril. Those who face the reality head on and take the proper steps now will enhance their ability to achieve financial independence.

THE STAGE IS BEING SET FOR THE NEXT BULL MARKET

We are witnessing an unfolding of events similar to that which took place between 1979 and 1981. There were many then who could not believe our government was capable of such radical change. This time, as before, the government will go to great lengths to prove how hard it is working on our behalf. Expect a long debate with meetings, hearings, and late night and weekend working sessions. After all, these changes will be historic, and the politicians will desire to reap all the credit—and spread all the blame. This dialogue will rage throughout the next several years and the issues will be hotly debated by both political parties. But our government has now embarked upon a path from which there is no return. In the end, economic policies will be enacted that will fly in the face of political and economic experience, but that could once more unleash the productive potential of the U.S. economy.

Meaningful tax reform and the containment of government spending growth by finally addressing entitlements in a realistic way will give investors the legitimate expectation that over the long term, with growth, budget deficits will be shrinking in absolute as well as relative terms.

There may be a difference, however, in the way the equity market responds to this scenario. As we discussed in the preceding chapter, a full year passed after legislation was signed in 1981 before most Americans understood the implications of tax reform for the financial markets. As a consequence, many investors failed to take full advantage of the investment opportunities that lay ahead of them.

This time, it may be different. We have that experience be-hind us. When we least expect it—the economic expansion may seem to be stalling, corporate profitability may be on the de-cline, unemployment may be increasing, consumer and in-vestor confidence may be on the wane—as investors begin to realize that this is indeed the direction in which policy is headed, and *before* legislation is signed, the U.S. equity market will explode.

The average investor, if he or she is lucky, will experience an economic and market climate like the one that existed during the 1980s once in a lifetime. Thanks to a rare set of economic and political circumstances, those who started investing in the early 1980s and are still doing so today will experience this phenomenon twice. In any event, few of us can afford to pass up the chance to take advantage of this impending opportunity. It may be the last chance we have to secure financial indepen-dence as we enter the twenty-first century.

CARPE DIEM: SEIZE THE DAY!

To sum up, the next bull market in stocks in the United States will be determined by exactly the same set of forces that deter-mined the bull market of the 1980s, and I would expect the po-tential for investors to be just as great. As a matter of fact, we are entering this new economic era in better fundamental shape than we entered the 1980s. Corporate restructuring in the early 1990s, as corporations desperately sought to contain costs and improve productivity, has once again restored their international competitiveness. Labor productivity is growing more strongly, unit labor costs are contained, interest rates are trending lower, and inflation, after years of a market-oriented monetary policy, has been restored to rates not seen since the 1950s and 1960s.

With our government on a path toward removing the only real threat to our economic well-being, the federal budget

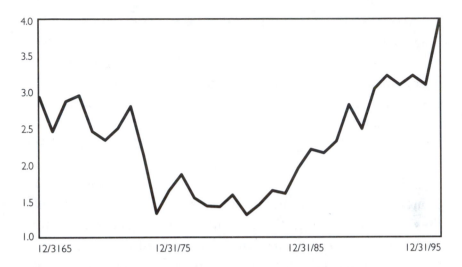

FIGURE 4.3 When the cost of living was rising faster than the stock market in the late 1960s and throughout the 1970s, investors as a whole were not increasing their wealth as fast as inflation was taking it away. However, during the 1980s and early 1990s, when market gains exceeded inflation, investors were able to make significant progress. (Sources: Consumer Price Index, S&P 500 Index)

deficit problem, investors should now begin to set their course for financial independence. During the 1970s, as a result of the prevailing economic philosophy, we experienced a commodity inflation and a financial assets deflation. In contrast, what we may very well experience as we enter the next century as a consequence of the new economic philosophy is a commodity deflation and financial asset inflation.

Figure 4.3 illustrates my contention that we are now experiencing a most impressive trend of the prices of financial assets (stocks) relative to the prices of real assets (commodities). One easy way to monitor that trend is to look at the relationship between the Standard & Poor's 500 Index and inflation as measured by the Consumer Price Index. At its low point in 1981, the S&P 500 was less than 1.30 times as high as the Consumer

Price Index. A basket of stocks was worth 1.30 baskets of consumer goods.

The 1981 low for stocks followed a dispiriting period that began in 1966, when the prices of commodities began to rise at increasing rates while the prices of shares of common stock meandered in the wilderness. At its peak in January 1966, the S&P 500 stood at 2.91 times the Consumer Price Index. That is to say, that same basket of stocks purchased more than twice as many goods as in 1981. Alternatively, measured in goods, rather than in dollars, between 1966 and 1981 stocks lost nearly 55 percent of their value. By the end of 1990, stocks had come almost all the way back. Since then, equities have outpaced inflation and this trend will only be enhanced by the new economic philosophy.

To put my expectations into perspective, and I must emphasize that this is not a forecast: if the next bull market were to begin with the Dow Jones Industrial Average at 4000 (which would imply a severe market correction from its December 1995 level) and if the market simply duplicated its performance between August 1982 and August 1987, it would imply a Dow at a level of 14,000 five years later.

If that level seems preposterous, consider the following. In 1966, the Dow reached 1000 for the first time. The 225-stock Nikkei Index, widely accepted as the proxy for the Japanese stock market, stood at 1364. By 1989, because of the proper economic conditions, the Nikkei pierced the 39,000 level. The reorientation of U.S. economic policy now taking place is setting the stage for the next bull market. We cannot afford to miss the next bull market in stocks. To do so would be like watching a football game, then losing money on the instant replay!

We may, in fact, be approaching a period of unusual opportunity. If you have ever surfed, you know that 90 percent of the time it is an extremely boring proposition. You sit on your board, facing the beach, waiting for that wave. You see people on the beach playing volleyball and having fun. And there you sit. If you pack it in and go join those playing on the beach, you are absolutely certain to miss the wave.

What I am suggesting to you in the strongest terms possible is that before you opt for the sand, just turn around. Look at what is coming, and get in front of it for the ride of your investment life. We are about to get an opportunity to accumulate capital faster than taxes and inflation can take it away.

I started this book by discussing its purpose. I have tried to explain how the economic system works and why the direction of economic policy is so important to the economic and investment climate. I have also discussed why economic policies may have differential effects on the financial and social climate in this country. I have highlighted the major problem confronting all Americans as we enter the twenty-first century: providing for our financial security without dependence on the government.

There is bad news and good news here. The bad news is that we are about to be set afloat to determine our own financial destiny. The good news is that, for those of us who seize the opportunity and take responsibility for our own financial future, the economic environment will be highly conducive to achieving our objectives. The rest of this book will be dedicated to navigating the financial waters in this emerging economic environment.

PART II

TAKING CHARGE OF YOUR
FINANCIAL FUTURE

CHAPTER 5

The Key
to Wealth

"Certainly, if a man will keep but an even hand, his ordinary expenses ought to be but to the half of his receipts; and if he thinks to wax rich, about to the third part."
—Francis Bacon, *Essays, "Of Expense,"* 1625

Saving versus Investing

Becoming financially secure in this emerging economic environment will require discipline and sacrifice. You see, to build wealth systematically, we must be willing to forgo current consumption. In effect, we must divert a portion of our current income from consumption in order to provide the potential for larger consumption in the future.

Now, I am not for one minute suggesting that abstaining in the present for the *chance* of consuming more in the future is easy or natural. Rest assured, it is not. I am, however, strongly advancing the proposition that there has been a sea change in economic philosophy in the United States that will dominate our affairs over the foreseeable future. And the economic policies it will spawn will make the economic environment conducive to attaining your financial objectives. However, at the same time, it will also make it mandatory for Americans seeking financial independence to develop the ability to exercise discipline in, and control over, their financial matters. In this endeavor, it will count for little whether one is old or young.

For purposes of our discussion, it may help if we make a distinction between savers and investors. While we use these words interchangeably, they really represent different people. Although both savers and investors must defer current consumption, it is the vehicles they choose to use to accomplish their objectives that differ. And, after all, as we will see, it is the vehicles that will ultimately determine our success or failure in achieving financial self-reliance.

Savers are typically risk-averse in that they are primarily concerned with the safety of their capital. Those who shun risk generally believe that the extra benefit of the dollars they might possibly earn with riskier investments is less than the benefit of the dollars they may lose. Thus, they usually prefer smaller, steady returns to erratic returns, even when the latter average out to be greater. Investors, on the other hand, are willing to assume some degree of risk to their capital in order to heighten the probability of increasing the return on that capital. While savers and investors may profess the same objectives, their approach toward achieving those objectives will differ dramatically.

Over the long term, the investor who understands the risks being undertaken and manages those risks carefully is the one who stands the best chance of achieving financial independence. There are no guarantees in life, of course, but to increase our chances of success, we are all now being forced by political and economic circumstances to become investors—to take some degree of risk. Failure to do so may preclude our ability to provide adequately for our future.

RISK: PERCEPTION VERSUS REALITY

If we are to assume risk, it stands to reason that we should have a clear understanding of the nature of the risk we are undertaking. Risk is defined as the chance of loss. But loss of what? Is it really the loss of our capital with which we should be concerned, or the loss of the purchasing power of that capital? Since the objective of a sound financial plan is to increase our command over goods and services in the future, one very real risk we face over time is the loss of the purchasing power of our money. We should not fall victim to money illusion. While seemingly obvious, it is worthwhile to keep in mind that what is important is not the amount of money we have. Rather, it is what that money will buy for us.

I am reminded of the story of the fellow who was 30 years old and well aware of the necessity of investing for retirement. But he did not have the temperament to deal with the ups and downs of the stock market. So he gave his friend $1,000 to invest for him for 30 years. In the meantime, he went to an island where he was unable to read or hear about his investments. Thirty years later, he returned and went to the first pay telephone he could find and called his friend.

"How am I doing?" he asked.

His friend responded, "Your $1,000 is now worth $2 million."

"Wow! I am wealthy beyond my wildest imaginings," said the investor.

Just then, the operator interrupted, saying, "That will be $50,000 for the next three minutes."

So, what we have to do is guard against that silent thief, inflation. As we have seen, inflation rates may vary over time, reflective of the vagaries of the business cycle and economic policy, but even relatively low rates of price increase can rob us of our ability to maintain or increase our standard of living. For those who are just embarking upon their investment journey, the task is to amass a pool of capital that will not only grow over time but, more important, grow faster than the inflation rate. For those who have already accumulated a pool of capital, the objective becomes protecting the income stream being produced by that capital from the ravages of inflation.

To illustrate the effect inflation can have on your financial future, I refer to Table 5.1. This table represents the amount of money required to keep pace with inflation. To see how much money you would need to maintain your current purchasing power, simply multiply your current expenses by the inflation factor you choose that matches the number of years you have to reach your financial goal. For example, if we assume that inflation averages 3 percent per year, in 10 years you would need $134 to buy what $100 buys today.

The insidious effect of inflation comes out in bold relief when viewed against the backdrop of the increasing longevity of the American population. A woman who retires at age 65 to-

TABLE 5.1 Inflation Factors

| Years | Inflation rate | | | |
	2%	3%	4%	5%
1	1.02	1.03	1.04	1.05
2	1.04	1.06	1.08	1.10
3	1.06	1.09	1.12	1.16
4	1.08	1.13	1.17	1.22
5	1.10	1.16	1.22	1.28
10	1.22	1.34	1.48	1.63
15	1.35	1.56	1.80	2.08
20	1.49	1.81	2.19	2.65
25	1.64	2.09	2.67	3.39
30	1.81	2.43	3.24	4.32

The inflation factors in this table represent the number of future dollars that will be required to purchase what a dollar will buy today. For example, at a 3% inflation rate, it will take $1.03 next year to buy what $1.00 will buy today.

day can be expected to live another 18.9 years (see Table 4.1 in the preceding chapter). A 3 percent inflation rate would cut the purchasing power of her income by 25 percent by her 70th birthday and in half when she turns 83. I am using this example only to point out that capital loss, while perhaps the most obvious concern, is not necessarily the only concern to be addressed in developing a plan for financial independence.

THE RISK OF "PLAYING IT SAFE"

Suffice it to say that there is no *safe* way to build wealth. And now that the government is systematically dismantling the structure of entitlement programs, whether we like it or not, risk will become our constant companion. Although we may be enticed into using certain vehicles that seem safe or guaranteed, there may be hidden risks. You know, it is one thing to take a risk of which you are aware, but it is quite another to take a risk of which you are not aware. Savers are especially vulnerable to taking on risks without knowing it.

Normally, when risk is assumed, it is with the intention of reaping a reward that is commensurate with the risk. Unfortunately, most savers unknowingly assume risk where the rewards are not commensurate with the degree of that risk. Although we may believe we are "playing it safe," our perception of the risk we are assuming may be different from the reality.

For example, many people, fearful of risking their capital, lend their money to banks in the form of certificates of deposit (CDs). These certificates are federally insured up to $100,000 and pay a stated rate of interest for a specific period of time. While CD rates may appear attractive at the time of purchase, who is to say what these rates will be over the long run? To illustrate, the average rate for six-month CDs from 1988 to 1990 was 8.4 percent, but the average rate over the next three years was only 3.7 percent. The return of the capital may be guaranteed, but there is no assurance that the return *on* the capital will be the same when the CDs mature and it is time to reinvest. The variability of these short-term rates highlights the *reinvestment risk* that savers are assuming.

Certificates of deposit and other fixed-income vehicles such as corporate bonds and U.S. Treasury securities (which pay a stated rate of interest for a longer period of time, with the return of principal assured at maturity) carry another risk to savers that may not be self evident. For those individuals who spend the interest from these securities as it is earned, the principal and interest will continually be losing value to inflation.

Suppose a saver buys a 10-year bond for $10,000 with an interest rate of 7 percent. This means a guaranteed income of $700 a year on the $10,000 for the next 10 years, then a return of the original principal at the end of the 10 years. If inflation averages 3 percent a year, the purchasing power of the $700 is declining each year the bond is held. At the end of the 10 years, when it is time to reinvest the principal, interest rates would have to rise 1.34 times to provide the equivalent purchasing power that the $700 annual interest payment provided when the bond was purchased, which means a rate of 9.38 percent. Ironically, savers who see themselves as cautious and prudent with their capital, unwittingly become gamblers on interest rates.

Meanwhile, the purchasing power of the original $10,000 would shrink by nearly 25 percent, purchasing only what $7,500 would have bought when the bond was issued 10 years earlier. Looking at it another way, your principal would have to grow to $13,400 to provide the same buying power as the $10,000 had provided 10 years earlier. But at maturity, all you will receive is your initial $10,000. If held to maturity, bonds do not possess the potential for growth of capital.

Bonds and CDs became popular instruments of wealth accumulation during the late 1970s and early 1980s as interest rates

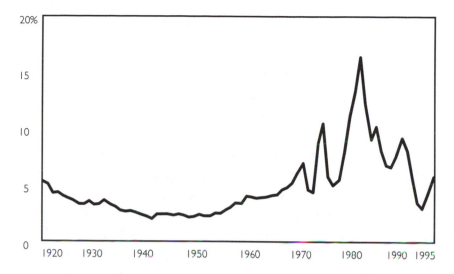

FIGURE 5.1 Yields on long-term U.S. Treasury bonds since 1920 provide a profile of interest rates over most of the 20th century. (Sources: Survey of Current Business, U.S. Commerce Department)

soared to historic levels. What was considered "normal," however, was really an aberration reflective of misguided economic policy. This aberration becomes vividly apparent when placed in historic perspective. Figure 5.1 shows the historical profile of interest rates in the United States. It is clear that the 1975–1985 experience was indeed the exception, not the rule. Those who relied exclusively on these vehicles were sorely disappointed as interest rates began their descent to more normal levels.

I should point out that savers who do not spend the interest, but allow it to compound instead, while still assuming the reinvestment risk, do stand a chance of keeping even with inflation and may even pull slightly ahead of it. But, as I will demonstrate later, the growth potential of money placed in such savings vehicles as CDs and bonds is strictly limited and generally does not compare with that placed in common stock investments.

M A R K E T   R I S K :   S A V E R S   B E W A R E

Savers may also utilize U.S. Treasury securities in the belief that because they are guaranteed by the U.S. government, they are completely safe. What many savers do not realize is that while interest and principal are guaranteed by the U.S. government, the market price of the securities is not. If you can afford to buy and hold a government security until it matures and your principal is returned, you will not lose principal or interest. However, if you must sell the security before it matures, you will not get all of your principal back if bond prices have declined. On the brighter side, if bond prices have risen, you may get even more money back than you invested. The situation arises in either case because the guarantee does not extend to the price of the security, which will fluctuate on the open market between the time the security is issued and the time it matures.

Since the interest payment is fixed for the life of the bond, if interest rates in the open market rise or fall, the only way these securities can remain competitive is if their price rises or falls. If interest rates rise, the price of the bond will fall to adjust the yield of the bond to market conditions. Similarly, should interest rates fall, bond prices will rise, reducing the yield on the security. Thus, interest rates and bond prices move in opposite directions.

Corporate bonds, likewise, will vary in price over their life, so you also face a market risk with a corporate bond—you may not get all of your money back, or you may sell at a profit. In addition, however, corporate bonds are also subject to *credit risk,* the risk that the company will default on the interest payments or be unable to repay the principal when the bonds mature.

Finally, those who save with CDs also face some risk to their principal if they suddenly need to redeem the certificates for an unforeseen emergency. The *liquidity risk* comes in the form of a prepayment penalty that federal law has imposed upon savers in order to protect the bank against loss if the lender (the CD saver) suddenly calls in the loan.

The message to savers is clear: do not be fooled by "guarantees." There is much more risk in these types of vehicles than may be apparent at first glance. The only "guarantee" that fixed-income securities offer is that, over time, you will increase your chances of losing purchasing power. Furthermore, since many Americans will now need a larger pool of capital upon which to earn income at retirement as entitlement programs are scaled back, these instruments do not possess the necessary characteristics to provide for the growth that will be required.

When you use fixed-income instruments like CDs, corporate bonds, and U.S. Treasury securities, you become, in effect, a lender. You are lending your money to someone or some institution to use, and in return they pay interest on it to you. By lending your money, you may achieve a good level of income, but you have limited the potential for both your income and your capital to grow over time. The only way to stand a chance of accumulating capital and increasing your income is through *owning* something. It is not that fixed-income vehicles do not have a place in a well-rounded investment portfolio; they do. But all too often, in the name of safety, people use these vehicles exclusively. By so doing, they substantially reduce their chances of achieving financial independence.

WHAT IS OWNERSHIP?

Let us now explore an alternative to "lending" your money: ownership. Ownership, or equity, is represented by such things as real estate, your own business, and tangible items such as precious metals and coins, or collectibles such as art and antiques. I think a word about real estate is appropriate here. During the great commodity inflation of the 1970s, home ownership emerged as a primary means of wealth accumulation for many Americans. Those who were able to purchase their own homes during the 1950s and 1960s were able to increase their net worth manyfold as a consequence of that inflationary spiral. The American dream had also become a pension plan. However, as the inflation bubble burst, home ownership has lost its allure as a means of building wealth. Increasingly, Americans are viewing home ownership as representative of a desirable lifestyle, but not as a means to financial independence.

For the majority of us, however, common stocks now represent the most convenient way to be equity investors—and the thrust of the new economic philosophy will favor equity investing. As a stockholder in a company, and therefore a partial owner of that company, you share in the productive potential of the enterprise as represented by the earnings, profits, and dividends it produces over time. I should add here that you also share in the potential losses. For a growing number of Americans, however, building a portfolio of common stocks has become the preferred way to share in the potential of the American economy.

It is never too late to become an owner of companies through common stocks. Most financial advisors, in fact, will tell you that even in retirement, it is a good idea to include stocks in your investment portfolio. The earlier you begin your financial journey, however, the greater will be the potential rewards. One reason is obvious: the longer you have to accumulate capital, the more opportunities you have to invest successfully and amass wealth. Another reason may not be quite as obvious: the younger you are, the more years you have to take the risks that may provide the greater returns—and to recover from investments that do not provide the expected returns, either because of your own mistakes or events beyond your control.

IT'S TIME IN THE MARKET, NOT TIMING THE MARKET

Time, the ultimate enemy of procrastinators, can be the ally of successful equity investors. Those who look at the headlines and say, "Things are too bad, this is not a good time to invest," then wait for better times, only to say, "Things are too good, this is not a good time to invest," will never grow wealthy. Believe me, you will always have a good excuse for not beginning an investment program.

Wealth is not built with 20/20 hindsight, but the past can be instructive, because the days that lie ahead will generate their own share of uncertainties. Timid investors can always find scores of reasons not to invest. In reality, however, investment opportunities often arise during the rough times. To delay an investment "until things settle down" may cost you potential growth. Figure 5.2 shows how the stock market, as represented by the Standard & Poor's 500 Index, has withstood the tests of war, recession, assassinations, market crashes, and other calamities. The reward for investors with patience and an understanding of the investment process: financial independence.

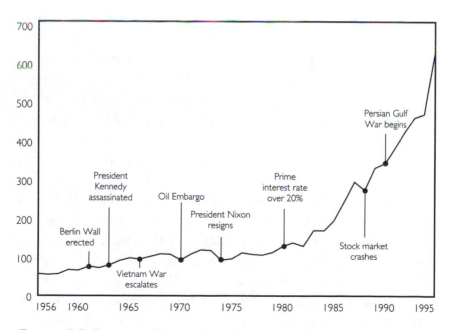

FIGURE 5.2 Progress of the stock market over the years suggests there has rarely been a "wrong" time to invest. (Source: S&P 500 Index)

Over time, it does not matter much whether you invest at the top of the market when dollars buy the fewest shares, at the bottom of the market, when they buy the most, or somewhere in between. Look what happens to these three hypothetical investors. Using the Standard & Poor's 500 Index as a proxy for the stock market, assume that beginning on January 1, 1960, Investor A invested $5,000 at the top of the market each year (bad timing!), Investor B invested $5,000 at the market's low point each year (perfect timing!), and Investor C invested $5,000 on July 1 each year. On December 31, 1995, the first investor had $2,197,167; the second, $2,615,866; and the third, $2,476,729.

Over the 35-year span, the difference in their investment experience is remarkably narrow. Furthermore, since it is virtually impossible to pinpoint the market's precise bottom, there is not much point in trying. And only the investor with the worst possible luck could invest at the market's top each and every year. The rewards for trying to *time* the market are just not worth the risk. The lesson to be learned from this example is that successful investing requires a disciplined investment approach without regard to when the investment is made. Easy to say; hard to do.

To illustrate further the financial cost of waiting to invest for retirement, consider the hypothetical situations encountered by two workers. One opens an individual retirement account (IRA) at age 22, investing the $2,000 maximum each of the next nine years through age 30, a total of $18,000. The worker invests no other money over the next 35 years, but leaves all assets in the account to accumulate and compound. At age 65, and assuming a 9 percent annual growth rate, a nest egg of $610,271 is ready to provide retirement income. The other worker invests nothing through age 30, then begins investing the $2,000 annual limit each year for the next 34 years. Assuming the same 9 percent growth rate, this worker's $68,000 investment grows to $468,393 at age 65, some 23 percent less than the other worker's. The early investor is the clear winner. This investor invested less ($18,000 versus $68,000) and winds up with more. The lesson: start your plan early.

In the previous chapter, I outlined the main reasons for expecting a powerful bull market in stocks as a result of a change in economic philosophy. The temptation to time the next bull market may become almost irresistible. The debate over tax reform, the vagaries of the business cycle, campaign rhetoric in election years, will all create uncertainty, increasing the temptation to wait until the dust settles. Forewarned is forearmed. If you try to time the next bull market, it will run right over you.

COMMON STOCKS: A PIECE OF THE ACTION

For millions of Americans, owning a stake in thousands of businesses is possible through equity investing—mainly common stocks and, increasingly, mutual funds that invest in common stocks. No matter how much we may take it for granted today, this widespread participation of workers in the ownership of corporate America is a fairly recent phenomenon. The seed was planted in the heady days of the Roaring Twenties. People of all income strata flocked into the stock market, seeking to make their killing in a frenzy of speculation that saw stock prices bid higher and higher with each passing day. That first wave of widespread ownership of stocks ended abruptly—and, for many, disastrously—in the Crash of October 1929.

Even after passage of a series of laws to curb the excesses that led to the crash, a generation would pass before Americans in large numbers would venture back into common stocks. Those who entered the market since the end of World War II have participated in the longest period of sustained economic growth in U.S. history, interrupted only by brief and relatively mild recessions. This prosperity was reflected in the rising value of equities. Even the recessions, which were accompanied by declines in the stock market, had their positive side for equity investors by providing the opportunity to acquire additional shares at attractive prices.

As we will see, the entire decade of the 1970s, when the stock market remained virtually flat, allowed investors who used a technique called dollar-cost averaging to build a solid foundation of investments for building future wealth. If you are not familiar with the technique, I will introduce you to it in the following chapter, and show you how you can use it effectively in your own investment program.

Investors who pursued a strategy of systematic investing in equities in the 1960s and 1970s were well set for the stock market explosion of the 1980s. Indeed, those who looked upon the sharp market crash in 1987 as an opportunity to buy rather than a signal to cut and run were rewarded for their foresight; within a year and a half the decline had been erased and the market was headed even higher.

The Importance of a Long-term Commitment

The point here is not that you should wait for the "ideal" time to invest, because there is none. Rather, the facts suggest that to be successful in building wealth in the future you must assume the risks that come with equity investing. If your goal is financial independence, you have no choice. And, once you have begun your plan, you should stay with it.

Like bonds, stocks are subject to price fluctuations, or market risk. Many people avoid the stock market because it is so volatile. They should be patient; time is on their side. Consider these statistics: the stock market's best year since 1926 (when complete records begin) was 1933 when it rose 54 percent as measured by the Standard & Poor's 500 Index. In its worst year, 1931, it slipped 43 percent. That volatility is what keeps people out of the stock market. But there is convincing evidence that looking only at short-term performance may be

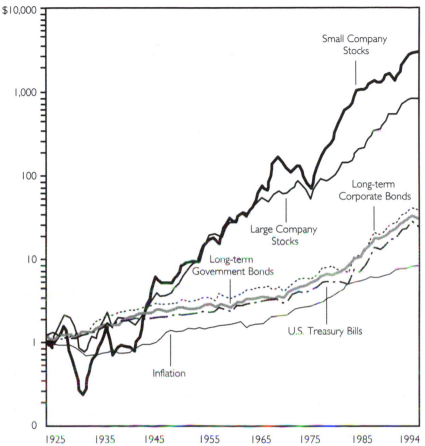

FIGURE 5.3 Chart shows performance of large company stocks, small company stocks, long-term U.S. government bonds, U.S. Treasury bills, and inflation from the end of 1925 through the end of 1994. Ibbotson Associates, used by permission. [Source: ©*Stocks, Bonds, Bills, and Inflation 1995 Yearbook*™, Ibbotson Associates, Chicago (Annually updates work by Roger G. Ibbotson and Rex A. Sinquefield). Used with permission. All rights reserved.]

missing the forest for the trees. The stock market's compound rate of return since 1926 is in excess of 9 percent, more than double the return on corporate bonds and more than triple the average annual rate of inflation. (See Figure 5.3.)

Of course, not many people have the luxury of investing with a 70-year time horizon. As you can see from Table 5.2, in

TABLE 5.2 S&P 500 Performance Over 1-, 5-, 10-, and 15-Year Periods (1928–1995)

Number of investment periods	Number of negative returns in investment period			
	1-yr. periods	5-yr. periods	10-yr. periods	15-yr. periods
68	20			
63		5		
58			1	
53				0
*Probability of negative return**	29%	8%	2%	0%

*Number of negative returns divided by number of investment periods.

the 68 one-year periods since 1928, there was a 29 percent chance of having negative performance. However, that probability decreases dramatically as the length of the investment period increases. For example, the chance of a negative experience was only 8 percent and 2 percent for 5 and 10 years, respectively. And, in the 53 fifteen-year periods since 1928, the stock market has *never* lost ground. The lesson: it is time, not timing, that makes for successful investing.

Discipline and patience are two characteristics shared by all successful long-term investors. These traits are not genetically transferred from generation to generation; they are learned. And given the likelihood that all Americans will be required to provide a larger share of their retirement income in the future, the best time to begin the learning process is now.

UNDERSTANDING YOUR CHOICES

Making the decision to invest in common stocks is only the first step toward becoming an equity investor. You now have to address such issues as your investment objective or objectives, your tolerance for risk, and the amount of time you have in which to achieve your objectives. Finally, you must find the specific investments that meet your own individual set of criteria. Chances are, unless you have plenty of time to devote to the task—and assuming it is a task you enjoy doing—you will want some specific guidance as you build your equity portfolio.

Because individual investors are increasingly finding mutual funds to be the easiest and most convenient way to invest in equities, I have devoted an entire chapter to these investment-management vehicles, so I will not go into them further here. However, as you will discover, with more than 5,000 funds on the market, finding those best suited to your needs can be a challenge in itself. Do not be concerned; as you will see, finding your way through this maze is not as complicated as it seems.

The most widely used equity securities are common stocks, which, as I have said, represent shares in the ownership of a company. Investors can choose specific issues for their ability to provide growth of capital, a stream of current income, or both growth and income. Preferred stocks, while technically equity-based securities, act more like fixed-income securities (bonds) because of their fixed dividend rates. The dividends on adjustable-rate preferred stocks are adjusted, usually quarterly, in line with interest-rate trends. Convertible preferred stocks, as their name suggests, may be converted into common stock and thus tend to be more volatile than straight preferreds. Because most growth-oriented investors place greatest emphasis on common stocks, I will confine our discussion to them at this point.

Growth Stocks

In general, investors seeking maximum appreciation of capital will look for common stocks that pay little or no dividends. Instead, the companies are reinvesting earnings for further growth or repayment of loans taken out to finance growth. As owners of these companies, stockholders can expect to share in the rising fortunes of these companies as they expand and become more profitable.

These small to medium-sized companies are normally found in certain high-growth industries conducive to entrepreneurial endeavors, such as computers, broadcasting, health care, and specialty retailing. Many companies in these industries may experience rapid growth. But in choosing stocks, you should also look for strong finances, well-defined marketing strategies, a commitment to research and development, and, most important, a management team with firm control of operations and an astute grasp of the company's mission.

As you might expect, these companies tend to be young and aggressive. Often, they are in industries that are also young and aggressive. Therefore, the stocks can present somewhat more risk than stocks of more established companies. Chosen carefully, however, stocks of these companies often can produce above-average growth of capital.

Value Stocks

Investors seeking growth of capital may also achieve it through companies that do not fit the classic pattern of growth stocks, yet nevertheless offer compelling investment characteristics over the long term. They may be companies that are introducing new products, making management changes, or experiencing earnings turnarounds. They may be companies operating in industries that are recovering from severe business cycle adjustments, or they may be companies of any size, including large, well-known corporations that seem to have "topped out" and suddenly come alive. Most often, the characteristic they share is that they are companies that have been written off by the market, which has not yet recognized the positive changes they have experienced.

Income Stocks

Investors seeking current income who also want their capital to continue growing will look at established companies that consistently earn good profits and distribute the profits to shareholders in the form of dividends. These are often large companies that are mature and no longer have great need to pour large portions of their profits back into the business. They may be medium-sized companies that have a secure lock on market share in the industries in which they operate. They are not as likely to be small companies, since these do not tend to survive in this competitive era unless they are growing—and committing most of their earnings to that growth.

RISK: NO PAIN, NO GAIN

You also have some control over the degree of risk you are willing to accept as you build your equity portfolio. If you are conservative in your tolerance for risk, you will likely be more comfortable with stocks of larger, established companies in stable industries. As a rule, these stocks do not fluctuate in price as widely as those of more aggressive companies or companies in fast-growing industries. You pay a price for this stability; the stocks are not likely to provide as much capital appreciation over the long term as those of the more dynamic companies.

I understand that seasoned investors may find some of the discussion in this chapter and the chapters that follow to be somewhat basic in nature. However, one of my hopes in writing this book is to reach as many of the millions of American workers as I can of all ages and in all stages of life who have not yet started to build the wealth they will need to assure financial security in this new economic age.

Many of these workers have not begun the task because, quite frankly, they do not know where to begin. Others who have started may wonder if they are going about it in the right way. Still others may be looking for new ideas to apply to financial programs already in place, and I am sure they will find some here. Finally, for those who are quite comfortable in the knowledge that their financial programs are on track, I hope this book will provide validation of that fact, or, if nothing else, will serve as a reminder that their plans should be reviewed and updated on a regular basis.

The secret is not to avoid all risk, which, as I have shown, is impossible. The trick lies in understanding and managing it. We have seen how interest-rate risk and inflation risk, often hidden from plain view of savers and fixed-income investors, can undermine the investment plans of the unsuspecting. We have seen how market risk and credit risk can make even seasoned stock market investors toss and turn in their beds. Table 5.3 summarizes the various risk factors inherent in the types of securities we have discussed. Of these securities, only common

TABLE 5.3 Risk/Investment Vehicle Grid

Vehicle	Certificates of deposit	Treasury bonds	Corporate bonds	Common stocks
Capital risk			•	•
Credit risk			•	•
Inflation risk	•	•	•	•
Liquidity risk	•			
Market risk/ interest-rate risk		•	•	•
Reinvestment risk	•	•	•	

Glossary of risk

Capital risk—The risk that principal will not be returned intact.

Credit risk—The risk that the issuer will be unable to make interest and principal payments.

Inflation risk—The risk that rising price levels will erode the purchasing power of the investment.

Liquidity risk—The risk that there will not be ready access to capital.

Market risk/interest-rate risk—The risk that the price of the security or that interest rates will fluctuate.

Reinvestment risk—The risk that the capital will not be able to be reinvested at favorable rates when returned.

stocks have the ability to provide us with rewards commensurate with the risks we are undertaking.

As you will see in the next chapter, the good news is that, once these risks have been exposed, they can be managed. When you accept the fact that you will have to take risks in order to become financially independent, and when you become comfortable with the idea that rewards can, and often do, exceed risks when risks are taken thoughtfully, you will be able to participate in the great economic and market boom that lies ahead.

CHAPTER 6

THE PATH
TO WEALTH

"It is with industrious nations, who are advancing in the acquisition of riches, as with industrious individuals. A great stock, though with small profits, generally increases faster than a small stock with great profits. Money, says the proverb, makes money. When you have got a little, it is often easy to get more. The great difficulty is to get that little."
—ADAM SMITH, *The Wealth of Nations*, 1776

PLANNING YOUR VOYAGE

In the preface to this book, I likened your financial journey to a voyage. I said you would need charts and a compass to make the voyage safely and successfully. In this chapter and the ones that follow, I will show you how to chart your course and set out on the financial seas.

One more caveat before you set sail: do not venture forth without a skilled navigator. The first rule in making your financial voyage successful should be: do not try to do it by yourself. If you do, there is a good chance that you will become lost at sea or your vessel will founder on a rocky shore.

The temptation to go it alone may be great, since there would appear to be no cost and no one else would have to know your business. But attempting to do so could be hazardous to your wealth. Don't be fooled into thinking you will be saving money; it could cost you dearly in the long run. In life, we typically get what we pay for; advice is abundant, and if it is free it may be worth nothing.

Furthermore, do not be tempted to take the easy way out and adopt someone else's financial plan, with the rationale that it seems to work for him or her. You are unique and so are your goals, objectives, risk tolerance, and aspirations. There is no one set of directions that will apply to everyone. The only commonality is that we are all trying to attain financial independence. The means to that end will differ depending upon the individual. You should no sooner use someone else's financial plan than you would use his or her toothbrush. I cannot emphasize strongly enough your need for competent professional guidance in developing your financial plan in this increasingly complex financial and investment environment.

I am not saying you have to go out and hire an expensive and high-powered financial advisor whom you feel obliged to consult at every turn—unless, of course, you have an unusual situation, such as a family business, a substantial amount of inherited wealth, or a complex set of circumstances you find yourself having to resolve. However, just as you have a family doctor to help you and your loved ones maintain good personal health and cure your common ills, it is a good idea to engage a competent "general practitioner" to set you on a sound financial path, give advice when you ask, and conduct a "physical examination" of your finances from time to time.

Just as you would not draft your own will or go to court alone, you should not be reluctant to seek professional help in the creation and management of your financial program. The emerging economic environment will be rewarding, but it will also present us with new and complex challenges. A good plan, drafted with competent counsel, is one of the most important elements in assuring your present and future security.

FINDING THE RIGHT FINANCIAL ADVISOR: CHOOSE CAREFULLY

In guiding you in the selection of a financial advisor, I should first define what I mean by the term. To me, a good financial advisor is one who possesses a broad knowledge of the situations most individuals are likely to encounter in providing for their own and their family's financial well-being, and the ability to help his or her clients translate this knowledge into a well-reasoned, realistic—and attainable—plan. This advisor may be primarily a stock broker, an insurance agent, a banker, a lawyer, or an accountant. Or, the advisor may be one of a growing number of specialists known as financial planners, financial consultants, or financial advisors.

The point is, whatever description is used, the financial advisor you ultimately select should offer you more than expertise in a narrow field. Your advisor must possess more than simply financial acumen and investment experience. A financial advisor should be a good listener who can identify with your needs and desires in the development of your financial plan. He or she must be able to apply the right solutions to those needs and desires, and not be hesitant about advising you to engage other professionals to fill in where his or her expertise ends.

For example, it is virtually impossible to find sufficient expertise in financial planning, investments, law, and accounting all wrapped up in the same individual. Your financial advisor may be able to suggest that you update your will or consider a trust, but most likely you will need the help of an attorney to confirm the advice or make more informed suggestions and actually draft the documents. Your advisor may be able to suggest a tax strategy, but unless it is extremely simple and common-place, you probably should have a qualified accountant do the actual work.

You should consider your financial advisor, then, as the navi-gator of your ship, guiding it to port. But always remember, you are the captain; you decide the ports on which to call. Most important, the advisor you select must earn and keep your re-spect. Choosing one who is not compatible can cause you much lost sleep and do irreparable harm to your financial well-being. And "trying out" a succession of advisors in search of the "right" one does not make any more sense than continually shifting the investments in your portfolio. As with any other investment, it pays to investigate before you invest. Invest in haste, repent at leisure. Or, as any experienced carpenter will tell you, it is better (and much less expensive) to measure twice and cut once than to measure once and cut twice. I think you get my point.

Here are five key suggestions you should keep in mind when selecting your financial advisor.

Ask for References

Word of mouth from someone you respect and trust is an ex-cellent way to start your search. Turn to your friends and rela-tives for their recommendations. Ask professionals with whom you have worked, such as your lawyer or accountant, for refer-rals. After you have found two or three candidates in this man-ner, ask them for the names and phone numbers of some of their current or former clients whom you may call for refer-ences.

Be sure to make the calls, but also keep in mind that the ad-visor is not likely to refer you to anyone who will give a nega-tive evaluation. Be prepared to ask probing questions about the level of satisfaction, how long the client has worked with the advisor, how confident the client has been about the advice that was offered, how good the service has been, how compatible the client and advisor are. Keep an ear tuned for subtle negatives or for hints that suggest you might not be comfortable with a particular approach.

Check Credentials

Every financial advisor must be registered in compliance with regulatory requirements. An investment advisor who is charging a fee and offering investment advice is required to be registered with the Securities and Exchange Commission and also by the state in which you live. An advisor who is actually offering securities for sale must also be licensed by the National Association of Securities Dealers (NASD). Advisors dealing in insurance must hold insurance licenses granted by the appropriate insurance authorities, usually at the state level.

However, it might surprise you to learn that despite the need for licenses and registrations, the financial advice business is one of the most lightly regulated professions. In the current era of deregulation, this situation is not likely to change any time soon. Financial consulting is also one of the fastest-growing professions, where the entry requirements are barely more than having a phone and enough money to pay the registration fees. I must emphasize, however, that the vast majority of those offering financial advice are honest, sincere, and hardworking.

But I must also caution that these attributes are not enough. You need someone who knows the business inside and out, someone who can translate your expectations for a sound financial future into a workable and realistic plan tailored specifically to your situation. Such a person can only do this task competently after years of formal—and ongoing—training, coupled with plenty of hands-on experience. You have to determine up front whether the person you select as your financial advisor possesses those qualifications because, as I have said, a judgment error at this level can be costly, in terms of time and money.

Determining candidates' professional qualifications may take some pointed questioning on your part. Specifically ask what professional degrees or designations they hold. This kind of formal training is important, of course, and more and more colleges are offering personal financial planning as a major course of study at the bachelor's, master's and doctoral levels. But a good financial advisor does not necessarily have to possess such a degree; in fact, if any of your candidates attended college more than a dozen years ago, you should not expect them to have one.

Nevertheless, you should look for such professional designations as Certified Financial Planner (CFP) or Chartered Financial Consultant (ChFC). These designations are earned by studying such fields as investment management, risk management, retirement planning, and estate planning, and passing a series of tests in these areas. Be sure to determine that the designations are current. In order to maintain them, practitioners must meet certain continuing education requirements.

Professional designations such as Chartered Life Underwriter (CLU) and Chartered Financial Analyst (CFA) indicate more intensive knowledge in narrower fields of expertise, the former in life insurance, the latter in portfolio management.

Ask How the Advisor Is Paid

The means by which a financial advisor derives his or her income is not particularly important. What is important, however, is that you understand completely how the advisor is compensated. Advisors are generally paid in one of three ways: by fee (they charge a flat rate for their time and/or the amount of assets under management), by commission (they are paid based on the amount of your purchases), and by a combination of fees and commissions.

All of these methods are perfectly honorable and acceptable—as long as the advisor is up-front about disclosing them. You have a right to know exactly how much your financial advisor is or will be compensated. If you think the compensation is excessive, do not hesitate to say so. A competent advisor will be glad to provide a detailed explanation. After all, he or she is seeking, as you are, to establish a long-term relationship.

Make Sure the Advisor Can Serve Your Goals

None of the professional designations mentioned by itself can provide ironclad assurance that someone claiming to be a financial advisor is truly qualified or can bring the kind of expertise you need to your particular set of circumstances. Nothing beats years of solid and successful experience gained by maneuvering clients through several market and economic swings and dealing with dozens of individual situations.

You may or may not find such experience and expertise in a single advisor. But, if an advisor is affiliated with a multiprofessional financial advisory practice, financial services organization, or brokerage firm—chances are greater that he or she will be able to tap such experience and expertise. Therefore, it is important that you explore not only the candidates' qualifications, but the affiliations each candidate offers.

When interviewing candidates, remember the advice of Benjamin Franklin, who said, "If someone tells you of the great thing he will do tomorrow, ask what he did yesterday." Try to get a sense of how the candidates go about the financial planning process. Without divulging your own assets, plans, and financial goals, ask the advisor how he or she would invest a specific sum of money. A good advisor will refrain from making a recommendation before fully understanding your financial circumstances. Only after discussing your tolerance for risk, current financial situation, and long-term financial needs should an advisor recommend a strategy for you. Furthermore, an advisor must be able to tailor recommendations and advice to your specific goals and needs. The advisor should also be able to explain clearly to you the products being recommended and the rationale behind the recommendations.

Look for Compatibility

Determine whether you would be comfortable working with the advisor over the long term. To develop a successful working relationship with a competent and trustworthy advisor, you must be comfortable with the advisor's manner and approach. It is essential that you determine whether you would be working with an advisor who is sensitive to your needs. Would the advisor be available to meet with you on a monthly or quarterly basis if that is your desire? Does the advisor intend to consult you, offer you choices, and permit you to make the ultimate decisions?

YOU ARE IN CHARGE

The one thing you must always keep uppermost in your mind is that even though you have engaged a good advisor, you are in charge of your own financial destiny. By definition, an advisor is just that, an advisor. You are the captain of the ship and you must be absolutely sure to retain the ultimate decision-making authority. A good advisor will tell you this up front. A good advisor will also make recommendations and at times may become emphatic in pressing one alternative over another. Listen carefully; after all, it is precisely this professional advice you are seeking. But if you cannot be convinced, the ultimate decision and responsibility still must be yours.

The more likely case, however, is that *you* will be the problem. You may try to persuade your advisor to make your decisions for you. Your approach with your advisor must never be, "You decide." Instead, it should be, "Give me the pertinent facts, give me some alternatives, and give me your professional recommendations." Then you must make the decision, based on those facts, alternatives, and recommendations.

SETTING YOUR GOALS AND OBJECTIVES

Shortly after you have made your selection and advised the candidate, your financial advisor will make an appointment to sit down with you to begin drafting your plan. Through a candid fact-finding session, your advisor will be able to gather the necessary information to provide you with the services that enable you to define and implement a financial plan commensurate with your personal level of risk tolerance. Hold nothing back. Your advisor cannot do a proper job if you do not provide all of the necessary facts—and figures.

You should be prepared to discuss frankly and openly your goals, needs, and current and projected circumstances. If you are married, your spouse should be an active participant in the entire process. Insist, if you must; *both* partners should be fully knowledgeable about the family's finances, and *both* must be in concert with the goals and the means of attaining them.

The first thing you will need to do is to get a precise fix on your destination. As the saying goes, if you don't know where you are headed, how will you know when you get there? After you have determined your goal, you will need a good compass and a precise set of charts to show you how to reach it. The compass will tell you *where* you are going, the charts will show you *how* you will reach your destination. Your financial advisor will be able to lay out the best course to take you where you are going in the fastest and most efficient way.

Your advisor will begin by determining your current financial situation, then get a solid grasp of your goals, objectives, aspirations, and prospects for the future. From this information will come a set of recommendations about which routes to take to your destination and which vehicles to carry you there.

No matter how reliable the charts and compass are, however, they cannot foresee everything you will encounter along the way. Therefore, you will have to stop every so often to check your progress, make sure you are still on schedule, and adjust your course. We will go into the process in greater depth in a later chapter. Once accompanied by a competent financial advisor and armed with a good financial plan, you will be ready to begin your trip toward financial security.

At this point, it becomes necessary to distinguish between goals and objectives. Let us say that your goal is to become independently wealthy. Your objectives, however, may be shorter-term, or they may be smaller pieces that fit together to make up the grand plan. You probably will find that you must continually adjust your objectives as you work toward attaining your goal. For example, an early objective might be to start a retirement plan. Later, you might begin putting money away toward the purchase of a home. Once the house has been purchased and the monthly mortgage payments worked into your household budget, you might focus on putting funds aside for your children's education. Objectives, then, are "way stations" along your path toward your goal. They are places where you stop to assess the terrain, make any necessary adjustments, and chart the course for the next leg of your financial journey.

Objectives will also differ depending on where you are in life—your age and financial status. Typically, the younger you are, the more investment risk you can assume. In the early stages, therefore, the primary focus might be on undertaking a fairly aggressive program of capital accumulation. In the middle stages, the emphasis might shift toward protecting the capital already acquired, while continuing to build the capital base, but in a more restrained fashion. In the latter stages, the effort might center almost entirely on preservation of capital and enhancing the income-producing capability of that capital.

BUILDING YOUR CAPITAL BASE

If you are still fairly young, a prudent way to go about setting your financial objectives is to make the assumption that Social Security and Medicare will not be available. As discussed in Chapter 4, major reforms to Social Security and Medicare will return these programs to "safety net" status for most Americans. While some benefits no doubt will still be available, it is my view that you should treat any benefits you ultimately derive from Social Security and Medicare as a bonus. You most certainly should not incorporate these projected payments and benefits into your expected retirement income stream. As a result, you may be required to defer more current consumption than you might have anticipated in order to build an adequate base of capital from which to earn income when you retire.

Regardless of your life stage, however, your pursuit of financial independence will require knowledge and discipline. One way to go about the task of building an adequate capital base is to adopt the principle of "paying" yourself first. At the end of every month when you sit down to pay your bills, the first check you write should be to your investment plan. All too often, it is the last check to be written—if it is written at all—and the first one to go unpaid when funds are tight. But write it every time, even if it is for a very small amount. The key here is to develop strong habits and to make your payments regularly.

Dollar-cost Averaging: The Eighth Wonder of the World

By paying yourself first, you are automatically taking advantage of a strategy called *dollar-cost averaging*. Putting away a predetermined amount of money on a regular basis (systematic investing) is a proven way to build wealth. But it produces other benefits, as well. It frees you of the need—or should I say *temptation*—to time the market. The objective is to purchase an investment at varying prices so its fluctuating value will minimize the effect on the long-term cost of your investment. Here is why: the average cost of shares purchased through the regular investment of a set amount of money tends to even out the peaks and troughs of the market.

Your dollars purchase fewer shares when the market is up, but they buy more when it is down. The longer you keep investing, the smoother the *average share cost* line becomes.

Furthermore, over a long enough period, it makes little difference what the mood of the market was when you began. It is important to keep in mind that in order for dollar-cost averaging to work, you must have the financial resources and the resolve to make the contributions on each appointed date. That means swallowing hard and sending the check even as you see the market sinking lower and lower—and buying more shares that will grow in value when the market finally turns upward. Understanding the process will help you develop the discipline to stick with your plan.

Here is how dollar-cost averaging works. Let's say you invested $180 monthly in a mutual fund. You started with 10 shares at $18 each. The next month, the price fell to $15 and your $180 contribution bought 12 shares. In the third month, the price fell again to $10 a share, and your $180 bought 18 more shares. In the fourth month, the price then rose to $20 a share and your $180 bought nine shares. By the fifth month, the price had dropped again to $18 a share and you bought 10 more shares. Did you win or lose? You won. Here is why:

Total invested:	$900.00
Total shares bought:	59
Average share price:	$16.20
Average cost per share:	$15.25
TOTAL VALUE:	$1,062.00

Of course, this is a hypothetical example. But it shows you exactly how dollar-cost averaging can work for you.

To emphasize the effects of market volatility, I have assumed some rather wide swings in the market. Dollar-cost averaging cannot produce profits in a sustained down market, and it will produce less spectacular profits than buying low and selling high. But history shows us that the first condition is unlikely (see Table 5.2 in the preceding chapter) and the second is impossible. Nevertheless, systematic investing does remove much of the uncertainty and anxiety about *when* to invest, and it imposes the discipline that is required to persist in the implementation of your financial plan.

My own introduction to the concept of dollar-cost averaging occurred when I first became involved in the mutual fund industry in 1972. I was a professional economist, trained in the workings of the economic system, but knew virtually nothing about the investment process. On my first day on the job at the mutual fund company, I was told by professional investors who had been managing money for 20, 30, and, in one case, 40 years, that I had perfect timing. I had gotten into the mutual fund industry in July 1972 as the Dow Jones approached 1052, its highest level in history.

I was told that the only way to build capital successfully over the long term was to begin a systematic investment program in an aggressive equity-based mutual fund. Dollar-cost averaging, I was advised, was "the eighth wonder of the world." So I embarked upon a program of diverting 6 percent of my paycheck every two weeks into an aggressive equity mutual fund, and I was off to pursue my career—and seek my "fortune"—in mutual funds.

As things turned out, I did indeed have perfect timing. I got into the business—and into the market—just in time for the oil embargo of 1973. I watched the American economy literally collapse. I saw the Dow Jones Industrial Average plunge to 574 over an 18-month period, a decline of 43 percent, even if we include dividend reinvestment. After several months of that experience, I went back to these investment professionals, who had now become my colleagues and friends, and told them that their eighth wonder of the world was not so wonderful any more. It did not work.

They told me, "Bob, you just don't understand the investment process." These price declines, they explained, were allowing me to accumulate more *shares* than if prices had remained high.

I told them, "I don't want to accumulate shares; I want my money back." Despite my vocal protests, I did let my money run, not for 10 weeks or 10 months. I continued my plan for the next 10 years, investing 6 percent of my paycheck every two weeks. By July 1982, after a roller-coaster ride, the Dow Jones average was only at 777. I still had my doubts, but I stayed with my plan.

Then, as we have seen, as the result of a shift in economic philosophy and policy, the market exploded in August 1982. Over the next five years, equity prices soared, and I watched the value of my accumulated shares rise along with them. It was after that experience that I realized that those who accumulated wealth in the 1980s were not the individuals who had tried to time the market in the 1980s. Rather, it was those individuals who had taken the advice and had the discipline to use the technique of dollar-cost averaging during the 1970s. I will go so far as to suggest that those who will accumulate wealth as we enter the next century will not be those who try to time the next bull market, but those who begin a dollar-cost averaging program now.

When implementing a systematic investing program, it is better to take something out of every paycheck rather than investing a lump sum once a year. In general, the more frequently you invest, the better dollar-cost averaging works. You let the market's natural day-to-day volatility work for you. Figure 6.1 compares the results of investing monthly, once every six months, and once every year over a 20-year period. Dollar-cost averaging assures you of a rational and systematic approach, which puts no stress on timing. The point is that it does not matter when you invest in the market cycle. What matters is that you start your program.

The Magic of Compounding

When you use the technique of dollar-cost averaging and reinvest all interest and dividends from your shares, you also take

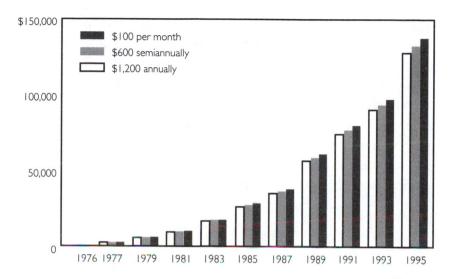

FIGURE 6.1 Chart compares the results of hypothetical $100 monthly, $600 semiannual, and $1,200 annual investments in the Standard & Poor's 500 Index over the 20-year period from December 31, 1975, through December 31, 1995. At the end of the period, the investor in this example who invested monthly had accumulated almost 4 percent more than the investor who invested twice a year and almost 8 percent more than the investor who invested only once each year.

advantage of the benefits of compounding. Compounding of interest and dividends is a process whereby interest and dividends are not only earned on the original capital (principal), but also on all interest and dividends previously accrued. To illustrate the tremendous power of compounding, consider this: if you were to invest a penny on the first day of the month and the value of that penny were to double each day, at the end of the month you would have more than $5 million. If this example is not dramatic enough, had Peter Minuit invested his $24 at an average compound rate of 8 percent instead of buying Manhattan Island from the Indians, it would be worth $76 trillion today.

These are just illustrations, of course, but consider this more realistic situation, using actual results: if you had invested

$1,000 in the stock market in 1928 and your investment tracked the results of the Standard & Poor's 500 Index, with all dividends reinvested, your account would be worth $707,486 today. If, on the other hand, you had spent the dividends as they were paid out, the $1,000 investment would have grown to $34,877, a mere 5 percent of the value with dividends reinvested. Truly, it is the reinvestment of dividends and the potential for these dividends to grow over time that leads to the creation of wealth. No wonder they call it "magic."

MANAGING THE RISKS

As we have seen, inherent in the process of accumulating wealth is the necessity of bearing risk. However, these risks can and should be managed and controlled. Here are several ways you can address the process of risk management as you build and maintain your investment program.

Invest Regularly

As we have just discussed, dollar-cost averaging allows you to manage the market risk: the risk that the market will be higher or lower than it was when you made your investment. Such a systematic investing program smoothes out the market's volatility over time and removes the temptation to try to time the market. In fact, it enables you to make the volatility work for you, especially if you make your contributions fairly frequently. This is because even in a rising market, you stand a chance of making your investment when the market is experiencing a brief decline.

In Chapter 5, we discussed the benefit of starting your investment plan early. The reason is straightforward. The more time you give yourself to reach your financial goal, the less risk you need to assume in order to attain it—yet, the more risk you can afford to take. Let's look at an example of two investors, both 30 years old. Investor A starts an IRA program by investing the maximum allowable under current law ($2,000 per year or $166.67 per month) and continues until age 65. If the investment were to compound at 9 percent per year, the $70,000 in contributions would be worth $493,975 at retirement.

Investor B, however, waits 10 years before beginning a plan and also invests the maximum $2,000 per year until age 65. Assuming this investment also compounds at 9 percent per year, the $50,000 in contributions would be worth only $188,255. The point here is not that investor B will have less than investor A, but rather, that in order to be as well off as investor A at age 65, investor B would have to find an investment that would compound monthly at a nominal rate of 14.45 percent per year. To achieve that rate of return, investor B would have to assume substantially more risk than investor A.

This example highlights an interesting irony: the longer you wait to implement your financial plan, the more risk you will have to assume to achieve your goal. But the less time you allow yourself, (that is, the older you are), the less risk you can afford to take. The longer your time horizon, the easier it is to manage and control risk.

Investing a predetermined amount on a regular basis also helps you avoid a common mistake many investors make: buying high. Human nature is often contradictory. As investors, we often do things we would not do when we go shopping for other things. If the largest department store in your city were running a sale with 30 percent off everything in the store, there would be lines stretching around the block to get in. When the stock market is putting things on sale, we don't want any part of it. Ironically, we seem to want to invest when prices are high. The only time you want the market prices to be high is when you are selling your stock, not buying it. In a systematic investment program like dollar-cost averaging, you buy your shares at whatever price they are selling on that day.

Chances are as good as not that you will get them at what later proves to be a bargain price.

Diversify Your Investments

Another method of managing risk is through diversification. As the old saw goes, do not put all your eggs in one basket. Your financial future should not be tied solely to the fortunes of a small number of companies or securities. There are several ways you can diversify your assets to spread risks. You can diversify within the same industry by investing in companies that will be competing with each other. This may avoid the difficulty of choosing the "best" companies, since the list may change over time.

You may also diversify among industries. The fortunes of various industries will rise and fall with the business cycle, and the ownership of companies in a number of industry sectors will tend to smooth out the volatility of your portfolio. Seasoned investors know, for example, that when the economy begins to grow stronger, demand will rise for consumer goods. They will invest in companies that produce the autos, television sets, and housewares that will soon be in greater demand. When the economy begins to slow down, these investors will invest in the companies that produce goods and services, such as food, insurance, or drugs, that are always in demand whether the economy is vibrant or weak.

Still another way to diversify your portfolio is to invest among the different countries in the world. Not only does this allow you to diversify among many companies, but differences in the pattern of business cycles can reduce volatility while increasing potential returns.

Finally, you can diversify your portfolio by investing in different types of securities—stocks, common and preferred; and bonds, corporate, government, municipal, and high-yield.

Your advisor will be able to navigate you through the various options to put together an investment program that suits your personal tolerance for risk, your long-term and short-term objectives, and the amount of capital you are able to provide. Within those guidelines, your plan should be drafted so it minimizes the risk to which you might subject your assets, while maximizing your potential return.

Buy and Hold

Invest for the long term. Just as market-timers rarely do well over the long haul, neither do "traders." It is important to distinguish between traders, who are constantly buying and selling stocks because they see opportunities or want to take quick profits, and investors, who seek out solid investments and stick with them, through good times and bad. In the end, it is the long-term investors who generally make out better, even if their portfolios contain stocks that make only modest, but consistent headway.

Traders must be right twice: they must buy at the right time and sell at the right time. Trading is a zero-sum game; for every winner, there is a loser. Traders try to take advantage of price differences and other inefficiencies in the marketplace that may exist for an extremely brief period. While there are those professionals who are right more often than they are wrong, the risks inherent in this practice are not for the average investor. And even among professional traders, there are very few who are consistent winners. Do not be tempted to trade securities even though you may occasionally hit it big. The odds are that you will give up the gain on the next try. Slow and steady wins the race.

Don't let the markets set your investment agenda. Remember, the prices of securities are printed in the paper every day as an accommodation to investors. But for investors who are in the process of accumulating capital, those prices are not theirs; those prices are for people who are selling their shares. Your prices will not be in the newspapers for 5, 10, 15, or 30 years. So, relax.

Take Advantage of Research

Many brokerage firms develop and make available research reports on economic and business trends and publish in-depth stock and bond recommendations on individual companies. While these are often technical in nature, they may be helpful to you in developing familiarity with the investment process, if for no reason other than allowing you to ask more knowledgeable questions of your financial advisor.

Read Financial Publications

Today, virtually every major metropolitan daily newspaper has an expanded investment section. I am not referring to the stock listings, but to the interviews, financial articles, and columns that can keep you up to date on emerging financial and business trends. Daily and weekly financial newspapers provide more detailed information. In addition, a number of excellent magazines have emerged that are specifically directed toward the average investor. Libraries in many communities subscribe to various investment-oriented newsletters.

A number of these financial- and investment-oriented publications are discussed in Chapter 10. However, you must learn how to read them selectively. For example, hardly an issue of the money-oriented consumer magazines goes by without a listing of the "best" and "worst" stocks, mutual funds, or this or that type of investment. It makes for compelling reading if you are interested in such matters. But it also requires care in determining what, if anything, you should do with the information in terms of your own financial program—especially those tempting stories about the latest "hot" stocks or funds in which you should invest your hard-earned cash.

My advice: read, enjoy the favorable things the articles are saying about the stocks and funds you have chosen and watch for subjects you should bring up with your financial advisor. Never make an investment decision based solely on articles written in financial publications. The fact that they are in print gives them an impression of credibility, but discuss their merits with your advisor first.

Maintain Good Records

Keeping good records for tax and investment purposes has always been important, but few investors devote enough time to keep their records up to date and intact. However, good record-keeping will ensure that you know how your investment is really doing and how well it is performing against your investment objective. One mistake many investors make that you should avoid is discarding records. Many financial advisors recommend that you keep all of your transaction records on file indefinitely. You never know when you may need a specific bit of information.

Monitor Your Portfolio

The days when you could buy a single stock and then forget about it for 15 years have long gone. In recent years, the financial markets have become more volatile than at virtually any time in history. As a result, long-term performance has become an increasingly important goal and the need to watch investment performance has never been greater. Do not become unduly alarmed by short-term fluctuations. Investing for the long term is still the wisest counsel.

However, you should keep track of your investments on a regular basis. Not every investment you make will necessarily remain in your portfolio forever. You must monitor them from time to time (perhaps an annual review would be sufficient) to make sure they are still appropriate for attaining your financial objectives. Companies' fortunes or directions may change. Or, perhaps your own requirements change and the investments are no longer suitable. Once you have made your decision after consultation with your advisor, do not hesitate to make the change.

Asset Allocation: Professional Portfolio "Management"

If this is all beginning to sound a bit complicated, it is because it is. The investment process is not easy and can be quite complex. Most people wish they had more time to invest their money intelligently. Unfortunately, blending assets to create an effective portfolio is not a simple task. While diversification is prudent, most investors find it can be difficult to accomplish. When they build their portfolio, they must select the securities from among what has become an almost dizzying variety of markets. The process does not stop there. Once they have assembled their portfolio, they must then continually monitor and balance it.

Investment Alternatives

Here are eight commonly used investment alternatives upon which an asset-allocation investment program can be built:

Large-company growth stocks	High-yield securities
Value stocks	U.S. bonds
Small-company stocks	International bonds
International stocks	Money-market instruments

Table 6.1 shows the performance of the indexes of these eight asset classes and demonstrates the difficulty in predicting the best place to invest in any given year. To help avoid investing in what could turn out to be a poor performer, you should begin with a blend of many different asset classes. This can lower risk and offset the volatility of any single asset class. Over time, a blend of investments that combine these different asset classes should produce more consistent results than any single asset class. Furthermore, the returns from a diversified portfolio, over the long term, can be quite attractive.

An asset-allocation portfolio appropriate for you will depend on your investment horizon, the degree of risk you can com-

TABLE 6.1 Asset-class Performance Comparison

	Best		Worst	
1984	U.S. fixed-income	+15.15%	Small-cap stocks	−7.30%
1985	International stocks	+56.16	Money market	+7.76
1986	International stocks	+69.44	Small-cap stocks	+5.68
1987	International fixed-income	+35.15	Small-cap stocks	−8.77
1988	International stocks	+28.27	International fixed-income	+2.34
1989	Growth stocks	+36.40	International fixed-income	−3.41
1990	International fixed-income	+15.29	International stocks	−23.45
1991	Small-cap stocks	+46.05	Money market	+5.70
1992	Small-cap stocks	+18.41	International stocks	−12.17
1993	International stocks	+32.56	Growth stocks	+1.68
1994	International stocks	+7.78	U.S. fixed-income	−2.92
1995	Growth stocks	+38.13	Money market	+5.37

(Source: Lipper Analytical Services, Inc.)

fortably tolerate, and your financial goals. Figure 6.2 shows three portfolios, each with different weightings of the eight asset classes shown in the figure.

The growth portfolio is designed to meet the needs of investors who are willing to accept a higher degree of investment risk and have a long-term investment horizon. This portfolio is designed to provide capital appreciation, with current income as a secondary goal.

The balanced portfolio is designed to meet the needs of investors who are willing to accept a moderate level of investment risk in their portfolio. This portfolio is designed to provide a balance between capital appreciation and capital preservation.

The conservative portfolio is designed to meet the needs of conservative investors. This portfolio is designed to preserve principal and have some equity exposure to keep pace with inflation. Your financial advisor can help you decide which port-

Growth portfolio

Large-cap growth stocks	25%
Value stocks	25%
International stocks	15%
Small-cap growth stocks	15%
U.S. fixed-income	5%
High-yield securities	5%
International fixed-income	5%
Money-market instruments	5%

Balanced portfolio

Large-cap growth stocks	20%
Value stocks	20%
International stocks	15%
Small-cap growth stocks	10%
U.S. fixed-income	10%
High-yield securities	10%
International fixed-income	10%
Money-market instruments	5%

Conservative portfolio

Large-cap growth stocks	10%
Value stocks	10%
International stocks	10%
Small-cap growth stocks	5%
U.S. fixed-income	35%
High-yield securities	10%
International fixed-income	15%
Money-market instruments	5%

FIGURE 6.2 Graphs compare the asset allocations of three portfolios, one invested for growth, one for balance, and one for preservation of capital.

folio is best suited for you. The more conservative the portfolio (the less volatile), the more the weighting toward fixed-income securities. But notice that even conservative portfolios (usually appropriate for older investors) have equity as an important component.

International Investing

As the world's economies become increasingly integrated and interdependent, investors should—I would even say *must*—take a global view relative to their portfolios. Many investors are nervous about venturing abroad, citing such risks as potential political disruptions, economic instability, and currency fluctuations. These are legitimate concerns, of course, and they cannot be ignored. However, as with the risks involved in investing at home, once they are understood they can be effectively managed.

Others assume that international investing is not necessary, in the belief that foreign markets move in lock step with the U.S. market. Quite the contrary is true, rather than moving up and down together, the world's markets are almost always out of phase with each other. A global perspective opens a whole world of investment opportunities, allowing investors to "catch the wave" of rising markets or diversify across a broad range of markets.

NEXT: YOUR "VESSEL OF CHOICE"

Successful investing, as you must have concluded by now, is not an easy task. Nevertheless, when pursued with thoughtfulness and care, and with a specific goal in mind, it can prove rewarding and even exciting, especially as assets begin to accumulate and grow. Fortunately, there is an investment process that meets all of the requirements for developing a successful investment plan. It is simple and easy to understand and implement. And, it is the subject of the next chapter.

CHAPTER 7

MUTUAL FUNDS: PRUDENT VESSELS OF CHOICE

"All that can be required of a trustee to invest is that he shall conduct himself faithfully and exercise a sound discretion. He is to observe how men of prudence, discretion and intelligence manage their own affairs, not in regard to speculation, but in regard to the permanent disposition of their funds, considering the probable income, as well as the probable safety of the capital to be invested."

—SAMUEL PUTNAM, Justice of the Massachusetts Supreme Judicial Court, 1830

ORIGINS: THE CONCEPT OF POOLED INVESTMENT FUNDS

The idea is simple enough. Several individuals get together, pool their assets, and hire a financial advisor to invest the assets and provide continuing supervision of those assets. It is so simple, in fact, that one must wonder why it took so long to catch on. But in the great scheme of financial vehicles, mutual funds are relative newcomers.

Even after the idea was initially tried out, a century would pass before those halting first steps would develop into a slow walk. In 1823, a New England life insurance company was organized in somewhat the same fashion as a mutual fund. A few years later, King William I of the Netherlands put together an investment program involving pooled assets that could be described loosely as the first mutual fund. In 1868, the Foreign and Colonial Government Trust was organized in London to provide "the investor of moderate means the same advantages as the large capitalists, in diminishing the risk of investing in Foreign and Colonial Government stocks, by spreading the investment over a number of different stocks."

In the United States, the Boston Personal Property Trust was formed in 1863 as a corporation in which a set amount of capital was raised and invested. The only additions to that capital were the dividends on the securities in the portfolio as they were paid and reinvested. In 1904, the Railway and Light Securities Company was similarly organized in Boston. In 1954, it enabled investors to purchase new shares and changed its name to Colonial Fund, under which it still operates.

In March 1924, more than a century after the first steps were taken to develop the concept of pooled investments, Massachusetts Investors Trust was organized as the first of the modern genre. Later that year, State Street Investment Corporation was formed, followed in 1925 by Incorporated Investors, now Putnam Investors Fund. These corporations all possessed the basic structure of mutual funds as we know them today, offering shares, prudent investment policies and restrictions, diversification, a published portfolio, and a straightforward and uncomplicated capital structure. They offered these features in an environment virtually unencumbered by governmental regulation.

By 1929, there were 19 mutual funds offering shares to the public with assets totaling about $140 million. Growth of this new industry was slow after the stock market crash in 1929 and during the depression. By 1940, total mutual fund assets amounted to only around $500 million. The tempo picked up during the next three decades, particularly following the end of World War II.

During the "go-go" years of the 1960s, as they came to be known in investment vernacular, when virtually every stock was rising, some investment managers made reputations as "gunslingers" by buying and selling wildly in this rising market, making huge profits for shareholders in their mutual funds. It was during this period, I believe, that someone coined the admonition, " Don't confuse brains with a bull market." So popular had the concept of mutual funds become that representatives were being recruited off the street to sell funds door to door.

By 1970, total equity and bond fund assets stood at $48 billion in nearly 11 million shareholder accounts, thanks in no small measure to aggressive sales tactics and the performance generated by the tremendous rise in the stock market. Were it not for enactment of the legislation regulating securities in the 1930s and 1940s, this marketing frenzy could well have gone out of control, as it did during the years immediately preceding the 1929 stock market crash.

As discussed in Chapter 4, the postwar investment wave crested in the early 1970s when the stock market, reacting to a hostile investment climate, took a nearly decade-long breather. Equity and bond fund assets, which by 1972 had climbed to $60 billion, plunged to $34 billion in the following two years, as shares purchased in the heat of the rising market were liquidated by investors seeking first to preserve their gains and later to cut their losses. Month after month throughout the 1970s, the Investment Company Institute, the mutual fund industry's trade organization, reported more redemptions than purchases of shares. By the end of the decade, as a result of redemptions by fleeing shareholders, the number of shareholder accounts had dropped to 7.5 million, and total assets stood at $49 billion, virtually the same level as when the decade began.

While the size of the industry was still impressive even after many years of net redemptions, it would look modest indeed after the more than tenfold increase experienced during the 1980s. It was during this decade that mutual funds became firmly rooted as the investment vehicles of choice for most investors of modest means. In the 1990s, mutual funds are increasingly being utilized by individuals whose wealth once was of sufficient stature to warrant engagement of a personal investment manager. Total stock and bond fund assets in 1995 stood at more than $2 *trillion*, divided among nearly 100 million shareholder accounts.

The number of stock and bond funds available to investors has also experienced explosive growth during the past quarter century, rising from 371 in 1970 to 4,789 in 1995. When taxable and tax-free money market funds are added, the total rises to 5,462. In fact, there are now more individual mutual funds than stocks listed on the New York Stock Exchange. It would be an understatement to say that among this dazzling array of choices, some funds are better than others. Choosing the right fund or funds to meet your individual financial objectives can be a daunting task. You can see why in the preceding chapter I so emphatically urged you to find a good financial advisor.

It is possible that 20 or 30 years from now the numbers we find so impressive today will seem modest by comparison. I would also expect that 20 or 30 years from now mutual funds will still be the investment vehicles of choice for most individuals. Why? Because, despite popular perceptions, a mutual fund is neither a stock nor a bond. To be sure, a mutual fund issues shares, and those shares have a price that is quoted in the newspapers every day. But that is where the similarity stops. What, then, is it? A mutual fund is a method of managing money. For most people, in fact, mutual funds may represent the *best* method of managing money. Technically speaking, there is no such thing as a "mutual fund." It is, in the truest sense as well as by formal definition, an "investment company." So, when you invest in a mutual fund, you are hiring an entire investment company to manage your money.

The Ins and Outs: Open-end or Closed-end, Load or No-load?

There are several types of mutual funds. By far, the most prevalent are *open-end* funds. These funds continuously offer shares to the public. Hence, they are also regarded as *publicly offered*. Another feature of publicly offered open-end funds is that they will redeem shares on demand. Because shares are simultaneously being offered and redeemed, the asset total is constantly fluctuating. The shares are valued each day based on the market prices of the individual securities in the portfolio. After certain adjustments are made in the asset total to account for management fees and other costs, the remainder is divided by the number of shares outstanding. The value per share, or net asset value (NAV), is published in the financial pages of many daily newspapers.

There are two broad types of open-end funds. *Load funds* are sold through intermediaries such as stockbrokers, banks, and financial planners, who charge a sales commission, or *load*, ranging up to 8.5 percent when the shares are purchased. *No-load* funds, on the other hand, are purchased directly from the issuing company and impose no direct sales commission.

In response to the attraction of no up-front sales charge, many load funds offer several classes of shares, in addition to the shares with the front-end load. The most common alternatives are shares that are purchased with no sales charge up front, but that impose a *contingent deferred sales charge* (CDSC). Typically, the CDSC will start at 5 percent for shares redeemed within the first year of ownership and decline by one percentage point each year thereafter until it disappears in the sixth year. Still another alternative is a class of shares that have a lower initial sales charge. A general characteristic of these funds is that they have a higher internal fee structure than the fully loaded funds.

Closed-end funds, in contrast to open-end funds, raise their assets up front through an initial public offering that is handled by an underwriting firm, usually a brokerage house. A fixed number of shares are issued and, except for shares issued to shareholders who reinvest their dividends, the total remains unchanged. After the initial offering, the shares of the closed-end fund are bought and sold on stock exchanges, just like shares of common stock issued by corporations.

As with common stocks, the price of a closed-end fund share is determined by the market, not by the underlying value of its investments (its NAV). If shares are selling below its NAV, it is said to be trading at a "discount"; if shares are selling above its NAV, it is trading at a "premium." Also as with common stocks, the broker charges a commission on the purchase and another on the sale of the closed-end fund shares.

I should point out here that occasionally an open-end fund will temporarily shut off new investments and no longer accept orders for the issuance of additional shares (not to be confused with a closed-end fund). An open-end fund's management may decide to impose such a cap for any number of reasons. Common explanations are that the fund is becoming too large to manage effectively, that there are not enough securities in a particular market for its managers to make sound investments, or that the fund is considering a change in its basic objectives or structure. Whatever the case, the important thing for you to remember is that if you are a shareholder in such a fund, in virtually all cases, new shares will continue to be issued to you if you have chosen to reinvest your fund distributions.

WHY MUTUAL FUNDS?

As mentioned earlier, the first investments that remotely resembled mutual funds were of the closed-end variety; that is, they raised a certain amount of capital, then managed that block of capital, essentially without adding to it or subtracting from it. They fell out of investor favor after the 1929 market crash devastated their portfolios. The few that existed during the next half century consisted mainly of closed-end bond funds, including a variant known as unit investment trusts. Closed-end bond funds are used generally as vehicles for providing a monthly flow of income. Unit investment trusts raise a block of capital, invest it in a portfolio of bonds, and make no more changes. As the bonds mature, the principal is returned to shareholders, and when the last bonds are retired, the fund is terminated.

After a half-century hiatus, closed-end funds made a big comeback in the latter half of the 1980s, when mutual fund organizations, working with underwriters (usually the larger brokerage houses), began organizing them at a brisk pace. They often were created by market demand for certain types of investments, and many have established credible track records. As with any investment, of course, they must be selected with care. Because of the diversity in types, styles, and performance records, however, you should consult your financial advisor before including them in your financial program.

From a purely investment perspective, closed-end funds and open-end funds share many of the same characteristics. Each represents the diversified investment of a pool of capital from many investors, each offers professional management with a stated objective and within a stated investment style, each must report to shareholders on a regular basis, and each may allow shareholders to reinvest income and capital gains earned by the fund. The similarity essentially ends here, however, since open-end funds offer a much broader scope of privileges and services than those offered by closed-end funds. Because of the greater variety and scope of open-end funds and the fact that the great majority of mutual fund investors use open-end funds, the discussion that follows pertains to them.

Mutual funds represent a method of investing that offers convenience and services few other investments can match. Whether you choose load funds or no-load funds, the basic structure is the same. The fund itself is owned by its shareholders. A board of trustees (sometimes called a board of directors) oversees the day-to-day operations of the fund and can make certain decisions on behalf of shareholders. The trustees "hire" the management company to handle the fund's investments, the service company to administer shareholder accounts and provide other related services, and the distribution company to conduct the marketing and sales of fund shares. (These separate "companies" are generally organized as components of a single investment management organization.) The trustees also hire and oversee the outside auditors and legal counsel. In some cases, the trustees of all the funds within the organization are the same; in other cases, each fund has its own set of trustees. Matters of a more fundamental nature, such as election of trustees and changes in the fund's basic operation or investment strategy, can only be adopted after shareholder approval.

Costs of running the fund are spread among all shareholders. The larger the fund, the lower the proportionate share of certain fixed expenses, such as administrative services, legal and auditing fees, directors' compensation, shareholder servicing, custodian fees, legal fees, and reports to shareholders. The fee for managing the fund's investments is computed as a percentage of the assets under management, typically starting at three-quarters of 1 percent and diminishing at certain break points within the asset base. But these costs are modest in comparison to the costs of operating other investment programs, such as the individual purchase, sale, and safekeeping of securities for one's own account.

Perhaps a word is in order here about choosing between a load fund and a no-load fund. On the face of it, a no-load fund might seem the better choice, since there is no commission attached to the purchase. However, a number of other factors must be considered. To get a true picture of the cost of investing in any fund, you must determine the total cost. For example, while a load fund may impose a one-time sales charge up front, it might have a lower internal fee schedule than a no-load fund. Although more visible, the one-time cost of purchasing the fund is not what will have the greatest effect on long-term fund performance; rather, it is the ongoing expenses. In the final analysis, what counts most is how well the fund meets the expectations you set for it in your financial plan.

Professional management is perhaps mutual funds' greatest virtue. Imagine the task you would face if you had to do your own research and manage your own portfolio. No individual can single-handedly provide the same consistent results as a mutual fund organization's team of professionals devoting their full time and attention to the research, selection, and execution of a well-diversified portfolio of investments.

Diversification is another major benefit that mutual funds offer. As every seasoned investor knows, by training if not by actual experience, the more you spread out your assets, the less chance you have of experiencing a major loss because of an investment's sudden decline in value. No matter how small the mutual fund investment, you have instant diversification, since each fund share represents partial ownership of each security in the portfolio.

Variety has become one of the mutual fund industry's distinctive characteristics in recent years as the numbers and types of funds have exploded. Your challenge will be to choose the right fund for your needs. With the help of your financial advisor, you will have to decide whether to invest in a growth fund, an income fund, or a fund that provides some of each. You will have to determine whether you want it to be aggressive or conservative. You will have at your disposal a broad scope of money-market funds for capital you may need at a moment's notice or as a "parking place" for assets you are still deciding where to invest permanently. There are index funds, which invest in portfolios reflecting certain indexes, such as the Standard & Poor's 500 Stock Index, and funds that concentrate on securities from various countries. Sector and specialty funds focus their investments in specific market sectors or industries. Believe it or not, there are even funds that invest in funds.

Convenience is another mutual fund attribute. Fund shares are easily and quickly purchased, and you may buy fractional shares. Once you own the shares, you may arrange for automatic reinvestment of income and capital gains distributions, or you may direct that the distributions be sent to someone else. In some cases, you may write checks against the assets in your fund. For many individuals, a very important question is, "Can I get my money when I want it?" The answer is, "Yes." If you wish to liquidate your shares, you may do so any day the financial markets are open. If you invest in funds within the same organization, you usually may exchange from one fund to another within the complex at minimal or no cost. Mutual funds make your financial record-keeping easier, an especially helpful attribute at tax-reporting time. Many offer consolidated statements for shareholders who maintain accounts in several funds within the complex.

Discipline in starting and maintaining your investment program is easy when you use mutual funds. Many mutual fund organizations can arrange for automatic monthly or quarterly withdrawals from your bank checking or savings account to purchase additional fund shares, making it convenient for you to utilize the dollar-cost averaging technique I discussed in the preceding chapter. It also automates the concept of paying yourself first. In many cases, you can reduce the up-front sales charge by agreeing to invest a certain amount of money within a specified time, or take advantage of other ways of earning volume discounts. In any event, if you pay a sales charge when you buy shares, you have yet another incentive to stick with your fund to spread the charge over a number of years.

A regular inflow of information about your mutual fund begins even before you make your first investment. The marketing literature extolling the fund's virtues must do so within the scope of a tightly controlled framework of rules and regulations, as we shall see in a moment. You must receive a prospectus before you invest, and once you have opened your account, you will receive semiannual and annual reports from the manager about the fund's progress. Statements showing the status of your own account will also arrive at regular intervals. U.S. mutual fund shareholders are among the world's best-informed investors.

Freedom from emotional involvement is a benefit of mutual fund investing that you might not immediately recognize. Many investors treat their individual securities like members of the family. Year in and year out, these investors will tolerate all members of their portfolio, good or bad and without reservation or judgment, long after these investments have stopped serving their intended purpose. A mutual fund's management constantly makes unemotional decisions about what to acquire, what to hold, and what to sell. All you have to do is make certain the fund you choose continues to meet your goals and objectives.

ALL IN THE FAMILY: THE BENEFITS OF MULTIFUND COMPLEXES

There is another context, however, in which "family" may make sense. By investing in a mutual fund organization, you have an entire family of funds from which to select when building your investment program and when exchanging among funds in the process of keeping your investment objectives in line with your long-term goals. In selecting a family of funds, you will have to examine the benefits, services, and privileges that are offered. You will have to assess the longevity of the management company and the experience of the various portfolio managers. You will want to look at the fund organization's record of service to investors.

In short, a mutual fund meets all of the criteria mentioned in Chapter 5 that a good investment program should have. But you will have to do some homework in order to derive maximum benefit from this increasingly popular investment vehicle. The best advice I can offer you here is that you must become involved in the process. Building financial security is too important a goal to be left to chance.

REGULATION: PLENTY OF WATCHDOGS

Earlier, I made reference to the securities legislation of the 1930s and 1940s governing securities and securities exchanges. Enacted in 1933, the first of these laws required all initial offerings of securities to the public to be registered and have a prospectus setting forth detailed information about the securities and the issuing company. The second, passed in 1934, established the regulatory framework for securities exchanges, created the Securities and Exchange Commission (SEC) as the regulatory agency, and directed the brokerage community to set up a self-policing body. The National Association of Securities Dealers (NASD) was incorporated in 1939 as a nonprofit organization for that purpose. Passage of the Investment Company Act in 1940 provided the basic framework for regulation of the mutual fund industry, a task that was handed to the NASD.

The SEC and NASD regulate the securities industry at the national level. In addition, each state has its own set of rules and regulations covering securities bought and sold within its borders. Even setting aside the state requirements, the body of rules and regulations administered by the federal government imposes a level of disclosure to the public that is unparalleled in the world.

In general, the securities industry adheres to both the spirit and the letter of the process, and in the great majority of cases, missteps are inadvertent and are swiftly and quietly rectified. Despite the cases that make the headlines, the consensus in the industry seems to be that self-policing through the NASD is preferable to direct involvement by the government in the day-to-day minutiae of regulation.

Within the financial industry, mutual funds are among the most closely regulated of all investments. They must be registered with the SEC and state securities authorities before being offered for sale. They must report to shareholders at least twice during each fiscal year. Open-end funds must update their prospectuses annually, issue supplements each time they make any significant change, and provide a copy of the prospectus to each prospective shareholder. In a real sense, an investment company operates in a fishbowl. Every move is exposed and can be scrutinized and examined by the public.

Marketing materials and advertising must meet a strict set of criteria that includes detailed rules about what they must disclose, what and how they may communicate to prospective investors, and how they may show fund performance in any advertising or marketing materials. Materials used in marketing funds must be filed with the NASD and cannot be used if they do not meet strict standards. While NASD rules are merely guidelines and do not carry the force of law, the body may issue sanctions against offenders. Egregious and deliberate missteps will be prosecuted under SEC regulations, which do have the law behind them.

In recent years, as more individuals have begun using mutual funds in their investment programs, the rules and regulations have become even more stringent. The focus of both the SEC and the NASD has been on assuring full disclosure to investors and the public and on setting standards of disclosure that make it easier to compare the performance of one fund against that of another. I can think of no other investment where so much information is available to so many people. I would urge you to take full advantage of this information as you build your financial plan.

The Prospectus:
Your "Owner's Manual"

An excellent source of information is the fund's prospectus. Each fund prospectus clearly spells out that particular fund's primary and secondary investment objectives, the strategies used to pursue those objectives, the types of securities in which the fund may and may not invest, and the potential risk such securities and strategies may pose. The prospectus also includes information about performance, expenses, and available services.

Before you may invest in an open-end mutual fund, you must be given a current prospectus. A fund's prospectus is its governing document. It states the fund's objective and explains in detail how the fund will pursue that objective. (Closed-end funds operate somewhat differently; like common stocks, which they closely resemble, their prospectus requirement pertains only to shares sold during the initial offering.)

The prospectus spends a lot of time explaining the risks of the investments it will use and tells you how it will *not* invest. In short, the prospectus is your "owner's manual." It is imperative that you take the time to read it. Most people do not, and that is why they are so often disappointed in the fund's performance or in its failure to help them achieve their financial goals and objectives.

When you give a mutual fund manager your money, you are giving the manager only that portion of your total capital that you want managed in a certain way. Reading the prospectus is the only way to be absolutely certain that the fund's investment objectives and your own are consistent.

In assessing your fund's performance, you should not expect a fund manager to go with what is popular at the time; the manager must follow the investment strategy as it is set out in prospectus. So, if the fund seems to lag the market or at times goes contrary to the market, the reason can often be found in the prospectus. As we discussed earlier, one of the features of a mutual fund is the ability to switch from one fund to another within a fund complex, should your objectives change. Do not expect the fund manager to do this for you. The manager's mandate is set out by the prospectus, and the manager will not (or should not) deviate from it. Only in this way does the manager have the potential to achieve the stated investment objective of the fund.

By law, all mutual fund prospectuses follow the same general pattern. If you are familiar with the prospectuses of one mutual fund family, you will not find the prospectuses of another family markedly different in their organization and content. Studying the prospectus sounds as if it will be a dull and boring exercise, but I assure you that one of the most serious mistakes investors make is not reading and understanding the prospectus. It should be regarded as the covenant between the manager and the investor. While at first glance the prospectus looks like an encyclopedia gone wild, it is put together in a simple and logical way.

The best way to illustrate this is to walk you through a typical prospectus. It is divided into three sections: the first tells you about the fund, the second tells you how to purchase and redeem shares in the fund and describes its features and benefits, and the third tells you about the company offering the fund.

I. ABOUT THE FUND

Summary of expenses. This section describes the sales charges (if any), management fees, and annual operating expenses that apply to the fund's various share classes. Information found here should be used to help you estimate the impact of transaction costs on your investment over time.

Financial highlights. Study the table that appears in this section to see how the fund performed each year for the past 10 years or since it began investment operations if it has been in operation for less than 10 years. This information should give you some indication as to whether the fund has been able to achieve its long-term objectives.

Objectives. This brief but important section states clearly and concisely the fund's investment objectives. In order for the fund to be an appropriate choice, its objectives must be consistent with your own.

How the fund pursues its objectives. The strategy and tactics utilized by the fund's manager in pursuing the long-term objectives of the fund are spelled out here.

Risk factors. All investments entail some risk. Read this section to make sure you understand the risks that may be involved when investing in the fund. The section also tells you how the fund's manager seeks to limit the potential for loss in the management of the fund.

How performance is shown. Here you find the description and definition of the measures that are used to assess the fund's performance. It is important to remember that all data are based on the fund's actual investment results in the past. While these may be a guide to future performance, they should not be taken as a guarantee of future performance.

How the fund is managed. Consult this section for information about the fund's management, how the fund's expenses are allocated and paid, and how purchases and sales of securities are made for the fund.

Organization and history. The discussion found here will tell you when the fund was introduced, how it is organized, how it may offer shares, and who its trustees are.

II. ABOUT YOUR INVESTMENT

Alternative sales arrangements. Consult this portion of the prospectus for descriptions of the classes of shares the fund offers and for points you should consider when making your choice.

How to buy shares. Here you can learn the ways you may purchase shares and the minimum amounts required to open various types of accounts. It explains how sales charges are determined and how you may become eligible for reduced sales charges on each share class the fund offers.

Distribution plans. This discussion gives you information about how the fund determines and distributes the various fees and charges levied against each class of shares.

How to liquidate shares. There is a saying in the industry that mutual fund shares are bought to be sold. Ultimately, shareholders will liquidate some of their holdings, and in this section you can learn how to redeem shares of the fund.

How to exchange shares. Your investment objectives may change over time, and in this discussion you can find out how you may exchange shares of the fund for shares of other funds within the same family. If it is a load fund, the section also explains how exchanges can be made without sales charges and the conditions under which sales charges or adjustments may be required.

How the fund values shares. This section explains how the fund determines the value of the shares presented for redemption.

How the fund makes distributions to shareholders; tax information. Here you can find a discussion of the various options you have in choosing how to receive dividends and other money earned by the fund's investments. It also discusses the federal tax status of the fund's income and counsels shareholders to seek specific advice about their own situation.

III. ABOUT THE FUND'S ISSUER

The final portion of the prospectus will provide information about the organization that provides the marketing, investment management, and shareholder account services to its funds and their shareholders.

THE SHAREHOLDER REPORT: UPDATE FROM MANAGEMENT

Annual and semiannual reports also contain much useful information. While the prospectus spells out the framework under which a fund must operate, its shareholder reports give you a more precise picture of how the fund was actually managed under specific economic conditions and during a specified period of time.

By regulation, each fund's shareholder report must contain a review of the economic and market conditions that prevailed during the period, a statistical review of performance during the period, and a discussion of how the fund pursued its investment strategy during the period.

Each annual and semiannual shareholder report also includes a portfolio listing and complete financial statements. Portfolios, in particular, can yield important information about a fund's strategy, including asset allocation, bond maturities, and industry emphasis.

Understanding Your Fund's Objective, Strategy, and Performance

Any analysis of a mutual fund's performance should begin with an examination of the fund's investment objective and strategy. Of course, the actual performance of the fund will be important in assessing suitability, but it cannot be used in isolation in making your decision. It must be viewed in light of the fund's objective and strategy. Understanding the fund's objective and strategies will give you a good idea of how the fund is *designed* to perform, against which you can judge how the fund *actually* performs.

Investment objectives can be grouped into three major categories: income, growth, or both. Investment strategies run the gamut from conservative to aggressive. A fund's goal is to produce results consistent with the investment objectives stated in its prospectus—for example, high current income or long-term growth of capital. Closely linked with a fund's objective is its strategy, which reflects the techniques used to manage the fund and the philosophies that guide it. The strategy is also reflected in the types of securities a fund buys, because different securities offer different combinations of potential risk and reward.

Assessing the strategies a fund uses to achieve its objective may be even more important in evaluating the fund's performance than the fund's statistical record. Why? Because you have to be comfortable with how the fund achieves its performance. To generate its results, the fund may be taking risks you as an investor are unwilling to take. Conversely, a fund may have generated superior results without taking above-average risk. You won't know, though, unless you examine the strategies and tactics used by the fund to produce its track record. Investors are comfortable with a wide range of risks depending on personal tastes. That is why comparing mutual funds solely on a statistical basis—in other words, picking the highest return—gives you little idea of how appropriate a fund may be for you.

Here is a way to help you judge a fund's prospects and ability to achieve its stated results (your financial advisor should be able to help you obtain the necessary performance data). Take a fund's 40-year record and break it into 5-year, 10-year, and 15-year periods (see Table 7.1). Then, eliminate the best and worst periods' performances and compute the average results for the remaining periods. The answer will give you an idea—but not a guarantee—of what you can expect from the fund over time. It will also tell you whether the fund has achieved its stated objective in the past.

A long-term investor should have at least a five-year time horizon; anything shorter than that may not provide sufficient time for market swings to be neutralized. In other words, a five-year period dominated by a stock market advance might give you an unduly optimistic picture of the fund's performance and, conversely, a period dominated by a market decline may hide a fund's true long-term potential.

Assessing mutual fund performance is a challenging task, but as you can see, it is not for lack of information. A veritable mountain of data is produced each month by a small army of

TABLE 7.1 Performance of The George Putnam Fund of Boston Over 1-, 5-, 10-, and 15-Year Periods (1955–1995)

Year end	Average annual rate of return*				Year end	Average annual rate of return*			
	1 yr.	5 yr.	10 yr.	15 yr.		1 yr.	5 yr.	10 yr.	15 yr.
1955									
1956	−0.78				1976	17.09	3.81	6.05	5.30
1957	−12.19				1977	−9.15	−0.65	3.86	5.93
1958	26.65				1978	−0.07	2.88	3.42	5.50
1959	5.53				1979	8.31	11.62	5.58	5.71
1960	2.81	8.68			1980	10.48	10.00	6.97	5.96
1961	17.17	12.36			1981	0.22	6.64	5.84	6.67
1962	−16.94	11.12			1982	27.96	14.21	7.16	7.63
1963	6.26	7.29			1983	8.36	16.08	9.92	7.90
1964	5.12	7.20			1984	−7.83	12.40	12.67	8.23
1965	6.62	7.99	8.98		1985	22.35	14.71	13.00	9.93
1966	−9.28	2.60	8.01		1986	12.02	17.29	12.50	9.96
1967	11.94	8.92	10.66		1987	−2.22	11.14	13.33	8.90
1968	4.26	8.50	8.53		1988	5.62	10.58	13.97	10.58
1969	−11.92	4.72	6.59		1989	16.51	15.88	14.80	14.18
1970	−3.09	2.74	5.96	7.28	1990	−6.61	9.79	12.89	12.36
1971	11.51	7.06	5.43	8.12	1991	15.72	10.51	14.52	12.28
1972	13.14	7.30	8.74	9.96	1992	1.74	11.39	11.93	13.13
1973	−16.07	2.74	6.21	6.99	1993	4.53	11.16	11.53	13.47
1974	−28.01	−1.31	2.26	4.30	1994	−6.13	6.46	11.73	12.40
1975	18.82	2.81	3.38	5.31	1995	22.62	12.42	11.76	13.18

*At public offering price, assuming reinvestment of all distributions.

statisticians dedicated to tracking mutual fund performance for the investing public. Unfortunately, as you have also seen, much of that information can be conflicting and confusing. No wonder, then, that investors are having a more difficult time than ever finding investments that meet their needs.

Now that we have covered some of the features that apply to all mutual funds, let's take a look at the differences between the two basic groups of funds—growth (stock) and income (bond). This will give you a better understanding of which type may best suit your financial goal and objectives. It will also provide a guide for selecting the specific funds within each category that may best fit your own needs.

UNDERSTANDING EQUITY FUNDS

There are six basic types of equity funds, with varying objectives. *Large-capitalization stock funds* invest in high-quality, well-established "blue-chip" companies. *Growth and income funds* invest primarily in dividend-paying stocks and, like large-cap funds, are designed for fairly conservative investors. (*Balanced funds* are variants of growth and income funds that invest in both stocks and bonds, usually in approximately equal measure.) *Aggressive growth funds* invest primarily in smaller, less well-known companies in pursuit of above-average capital appreciation. *Global growth funds** invest in stocks from around the world, while *specialty funds* concentrate their investments in specific industries.

Equity fund investors should consider both performance and risk factors when comparing one fund against another. Here are some of the most important questions to ask:

- *What is the fund's total return?* Total return provides the most complete picture of a fund's performance. It assumes that all income and capital gains generated by the fund were reinvested and takes into account the gain or loss in capital value over a specified period of time. Total return thus represents the fund's true performance, which can then be compared quickly and easily with the total return of other funds having the same objective.
- *How does the fund's total return compare with that of other funds?* Each fund's annual report includes total returns over 1, 3, 5, and 10 years (or life of the fund, if

---

*The SEC distinguishes between "global" funds, which invest primarily in securities from anywhere in the world and "international" funds, which invest primarily in securities from anywhere in the world *except* the United States. The distinction must be reflected in the fund's name. Hence, a "global growth fund" may include U.S.-based stocks, while an "international equity fund" may not.

shorter). To make direct comparisons with other investments easier, the shareholder report must also include the results for the nearest calendar quarter. Each fund's prospectus includes year-by-year total returns for the past 10 years. In addition, many financial publications publish comparative mutual fund results on a regular basis. Numerical comparisons are only valid when applied on a consistent basis. To be fair, compare funds over identical time periods, and do not focus too closely on short-term periods, which tend to exaggerate a fund's strengths or weaknesses. If short-term results *are* important to you, look for funds with the most consistent performance.

- *How consistent is the fund's performance?* Individual funds often post spectacular results over short periods of time, but one year's big winners often become the next year's big losers. Most investors will prefer funds that can sustain reliable performance over time. The more conservative you are, the more important consistency will be. A fund's year-by-year record, shown in its prospectus, will reflect its approach, as will remarks in a fund's annual reports.

- *How much income does the fund provide?* If your objective is both current income and capital growth, dividends paid by an equity fund will be important. Even if dividend income is not important to you, the amount of income a fund pays can be indicative of its volatility. Generally, the higher a stock fund's yield, the less volatile its share price will be.

- *How much risk does the fund take in pursuit of its objectives?* Risk, in an equity fund, arises primarily from the type of stocks the fund selects. Larger, established companies generally have steadier and more predictable earnings growth; smaller companies grow faster, but may face a less certain future. Stock prices reflect these factors, with large-company stocks being generally less volatile than small-company stocks. Over time, funds that take greater risks by investing in stocks with above-average growth potential will generally produce higher returns, but at the expense of greater fluctuations in principal values.

Equity funds are best compared against appropriate indexes or funds with similar objectives. Most professional investors use the Standard & Poor's 500 Composite Stock Index as the main benchmark against which to judge a growth fund's performance. The Dow Jones Industrial Average is better known, but it includes only 30 stocks and may not always reflect what the broad market is doing. The Dow represents almost 20 percent of the market capitalization of all the companies listed on the New York Stock Exchange, but represents only about 1 percent of the total number of stocks listed. Another appropriate index for aggressive small-company funds is the NASDAQ Industrial Index, which tracks the performance of more than 3,000 stocks of industrial companies traded in the over-the-counter market.

All three indexes are unmanaged lists of common stocks whose performance figures are based on price changes. The S&P 500 and the Dow also factor in reinvestment of all regular cash dividends, but the NASDAQ does not. No matter which index you use, understanding differences between a fund and the index is essential to the accurate evaluation of performance. Balanced funds, for example, seek both growth and income and are not designed to outperform the stock market.

UNDERSTANDING FIXED-INCOME FUNDS

Because fixed-income funds (sometimes called "bond funds") appear so straightforward, many investors may not realize that these funds can be more complicated to select and compare than equity funds. There are more varieties, with a wider diversity of features, income-generating capacities, and risk/reward profiles.

To compare fixed-income funds, or to assess the performance of an individual fund, investors should look at three separate variables: the amount of income the fund generates, the stability of its net asset value, and the quality of its portfolio. Each factor provides some indication of how well the fund is performing and, more important, how well suited it is to your own objectives and tolerance for risk.

The amount of income a fund generates is measured by its *current yield* or *current distribution rate.* Like the interest rate on a bank account, a yield expresses a fund's earnings from interest and dividends as a percentage of the principal. In other words, it is one way of measuring how much income your fund is generating on a yearly basis. Unlike a current yield, which is based solely on a fund's income from interest and dividends, the current distribution rate will also include earnings from such sources as capital gains and premiums from selling options.

The stability of a fund's share value is directly related to how much risk the fund takes. Except for money-market funds, which are managed to provide a stable net asset value (usually $1.00 per share), share values of income funds fluctuate in response to changes in interest rates, generally rising when interest rates fall and declining when interest rates rise.

The sensitivity of any particular fund to changes in interest rates is a function of several factors, including the quality of the portfolio's holdings, the thoroughness of management's credit research, the use of certain strategies designed to enhance income, and the average duration of the fund's securities. *Duration,* stated in years, is a calculation portfolio managers use to help determine how much the price of a fixed-income investment will rise or fall in response to each percentage-point change in interest rates. In general, the longer the duration of a security or portfolio, the greater its volatility. Because each income fund has a distinct risk profile, discussing these factors with your financial advisor will give you a good idea of how stable a fund's share price is likely to be.

In contrast to the case with equity funds, it is important to note that, for fixed-income funds, yield and stability of net asset value usually are inversely related. The lower the yield, the greater the stability; the higher the yield, the more variable the share price will tend to be. Money-market funds, for example, almost never fluctuate in value but usually have low yields. Short-term bond funds offer slightly higher yields but share values will fluctuate. Long-term bond funds offer even higher yields but have the greatest potential for price variability. Weighing this risk/reward trade-off is your most important task as an investor, since only you can decide if a fund's yield adequately compensates you for the fluctuations in principal value you are likely to experience.

Total return of an income fund is measured in similar fashion to that of a growth fund; that is, it assumes reinvestment of the income and capital gains generated by a fund and takes into account the change in capital value over a stated period. For money-market funds and certificates of deposit (CDs), which do not fluctuate in value, yield and total return are synonymous; but for most income funds, your total return will depend both on the combined effects of reinvested income and capital gains and the change in value of the capital.

CAUTION: DON'T COMPARE APPLES AND ORANGES

For many investors, total return is the ultimate measure of a fund's performance, but how significant it is for you depends on your objective. If you are seeking to accumulate capital over time, total return is indeed an appropriate measure. If, however, your objective is to produce income on which to live, a fund's yield or distribution rate may be more important.

At this point, I think it is important to clarify an issue that has been a source of confusion and consternation to many income investors. One of the most misunderstood concepts of income-oriented mutual funds is the manner in which they pay income. Most of us are very familiar with the way in which a CD produces income. Given the interest rate, the more money you have in the CD, the more income you will receive. For example, if you have $100,000 in a CD at 5 percent a year, you will receive $5,000 of income a year. If you have $200,000 in a CD at 5 percent, you will receive $10,000. In other words, the income is a direct function of the value of the principal.

A mutual fund, on the other hand, pays its dividends *per share*. The value of the fund at any given time does not determine the amount of income that will be generated by the fund. Income-oriented investors, therefore, would be well advised to focus on the number of shares they own rather than on the value of the shares, since it will be the number of shares that determines the size of the income stream over time. In a fluctuating interest-rate environment, the accumulation of shares is a way of increasing the potential for income to grow.

The quality of a fund's portfolio is another important factor to assess. Similar performance results often belie significantly different investment strategies. Some funds invest only in lower-quality securities that provide higher income. Generally, the lower a bond's credit rating, the higher the risk that an issuer may default on its obligation to pay interest and principal. To compensate for higher credit risk, lower-rated bonds normally offer higher yields. In-depth credit research can reduce the risks of default on securities held in high-yield funds, but you should be aware of—and comfortable with—a fund's portfolio quality before you invest.

When selecting or comparing funds, do not compare apples and oranges. Compare performance and results only with those of funds having similar objectives. Each of the variables I have discussed here should be an integral part of your comparison. You may also want to measure performance against a benchmark, such as IBC/Donoghue's Money Fund Average or the yield on bank CDs. One of the best measures of how well a fund has done is to compare it to funds with similar objectives and strategies. Performance against inflation is also important because it lets you know if your purchasing power is rising or falling.

When making any comparison, however, be sure to weigh differences between investments. Higher yields, for example, often mean a fund exhibits greater fluctuations in principal value, up and down, while lower yields often indicate greater stability. Thus, it is also important that you match a fund's risk profile with your own.

THE ROLE OF YOUR FINANCIAL ADVISOR

Your financial advisor is an invaluable source of information about fund objectives and strategies. He or she has access to a wealth of information from brokerage reports to investment newsletters about which funds may match your financial needs. Your advisor will be attending due-diligence meetings and doing other research about new funds. Before offering these investments to you, he or she must first check them out, ask questions of the issuers, and otherwise gain in-depth familiarity with them in order to judge their merits and determine their suitability for your financial program. Your advisor will also be in direct contact with fund portfolio managers and other key executives to gain familiarity with their management styles and techniques.

As mentioned earlier, the more information you can provide about your current circumstances and goals, the more help your advisor can give you. The final decision is yours, however, so you should ask detailed questions about how the fund is likely to perform. For example: How much income has the fund provided? How stable has the net asset value been? How much growth potential does the fund offer? What are the potential risks and rewards of investing in the fund? How conservative or aggressive is the fund in pursuit of its objectives?

NEXT: TAX-WISE INVESTING

Always keep in mind that income derived from your mutual fund investments, including capital gains realized when you exchange assets from one fund to another and fund distributions that are reinvested, is subject to taxation. In other words, the government is your silent partner, letting you take all the risks, then claiming its share of the gains. However, given the economic realities as we enter the twenty-first century, and in an attempt to encourage investors to build the extra capital they will need to retire financially secure, the government has provided many vehicles, such as individual retirement accounts, 401(k) programs, and deferred annuities on which income and other distributions generated by the investments are not immediately taxed.

As a consequence of the shift in economic philosophy, as we enter the new economic era, we can expect these programs to be expanded and enhanced and new programs to be introduced. In the next chapter, we will explore the opportunities these tax-advantaged vehicles can offer investors whose goal is to build financial security.

CHAPTER 8

AVOIDING THE TAX BITE:
SHELTERS AND STRATEGIES

*"When more of the people's sustenance is exacted through
the form of taxation than is necessary to meet the just
obligations of government and the expenses of its economical
administration, such exaction becomes a violation of the
fundamental principles of a free government."*
—GROVER CLEVELAND, second annual message, 1886

"Gimme shelter."
—THE ROLLING STONES, 1969

THE MESSAGE IS CLEAR: HELP FOR THOSE WHO HELP THEMSELVES

One of the most vexing problems now facing investors and one
of the biggest impediments to building financial security is taxation. Taxes act as friction on an investment; paying taxes is
like swimming upstream. The higher your taxes on income and
capital gains, the greater the difficulty you have in accumulat-

ing wealth. There are signs of hope, however, and one of the sources of help might surprise you. It is your government.

As Washington takes steps to make Americans more self-reliant, it will also help make self-reliance possible. Programs already in place allow workers to exclude from current taxes a portion of their income they set aside for their future retirement. Furthermore, they may also defer taxation on the investment returns that their capital produces while they accumulate assets upon which to draw in retirement. Existing programs may well be enhanced and expanded, and new programs may be introduced. I would urge you to take advantage of *every* opportunity to build wealth for retirement that the government makes available to you. Showing you some ways tax deferral can be used to achieve your goal is the subject of this chapter.

Before we proceed further, however, it is important to make a distinction between tax avoidance and tax deferral. Tax avoidance is achieved by lowering your tax bill in absolute terms, while tax deferral means putting off the obligation to some future date. Tax avoidance has become more difficult for most Americans because of the widespread abuses of the 1970s and 1980s involving tax loopholes and tax shelters. Loopholes are unintended tax breaks overlooked by those who write tax legislation. Once discovered, they are usually quickly closed. Shelters are deliberate tax breaks designed to promote certain activities deemed desirable by legislators. Often, however, they encourage the use of resources in an inefficient and uneconomic manner, and abuses usually arise out of the application of loopholes that thwart the legislation's intent.

So lucrative were the tax breaks available in tax shelters during the '70s and '80s that high-bracket investors could save significant amounts on taxes even if they lost every dollar they invested. That is why we saw oil and gas programs that drilled nothing but dry holes, cattle-feeding projects that produced no fatted calves, and movie deals that generated lots of motion but no pictures. Congress finally responded by demanding that such projects show economic validity in order to claim tax deductions for them. As a result, such tax shelters have virtually disappeared from the American economic landscape.

In recent years, Congress has also considerably limited the scope and extent of the tax deductions you can claim against current income. Nevertheless, there are still a few ways you can reduce the amount of income subject to taxes. Later in this chapter, I will show you some ways to make the most of your deductions each year. We will also explore the opportunities available through investments in tax-exempt municipal bonds.

TAX DEFERRAL: DELAYING THE DAY OF RECKONING

Let us first consider the most practical way most of us have for easing our current tax burden. That is by putting off the day on which you must pay your taxes. And I don't mean waiting until April 15 each year to drop your tax return into the mail. What I am talking about is putting off your tax obligation for years or, in some cases, decades.

While Congress has come down hard on tax shelters and deductions, it has taken a more positive approach to tax deferral. Legislators have been extremely diligent in guarding against abuses, mainly because a tax dollar not collected today is a dollar that cannot be spent today. Nevertheless, the result of what has now become a firmly established pattern is that nearly all of us are the potential beneficiaries of expanding opportunities to defer taxes on the income we put aside for our future financial security.

Make no mistake about it, Uncle Sam will eventually get the taxes you owe him and he will tax everything, including capital gains, at ordinary rates. But by providing ways for you to put off the day of reckoning, he is giving you full use of that money in the meantime. Consequently, you can allow your money to work as hard for you as you work for it. Remember

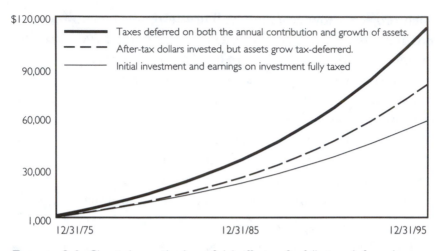

FIGURE 8.1 Chart shows the beneficial effects of a fully tax-deferred investment over an investment that is fully or partially taxed.

the magic of compounding? Watch how it works with the taxes you defer. It can pay to make Uncle Sam your witting partner, instead of your committed adversary.

Figure 8.1 compares the results over 20 years of three hypothetical investments of $2,000 per year, assuming an average annual return of 9 percent and a 30 percent tax bracket. The lower line shows the results for an investor who invested after-tax dollars, in which the interest and dividends earned each year on the investment were also taxed. Even if the investor had invested after-tax dollars in a qualified retirement plan that allowed the taxes owed on the interest and dividends to be deferred, the results represented by the middle line would have been significantly better. But the best results were provided by the dollars that were invested with all taxes on principal, interest, or dividends deferred. There are two lessons to be drawn here. First, it is best to defer taxes on both the principal *and* the return on that principal whenever possible. Second, if you are able to add after-tax dollars to your qualified plan, you will derive considerable benefit from deferral on the return those after-tax dollars generate while in the plan.

Evolution of the pattern of governmental encouragement of private retirement savings programs that we see playing out now began in the early 1960s. It came in the form of efforts aimed at ending the wide disparities in the tax treatment of pension funding that favored corporations over self-employed individuals. The result was the introduction of so-called Keogh plans. These plans allowed self-employed individuals to contribute a modest sum to their plan each year and deduct that amount up front before computing the year's income taxes. The sum was so small and the rules so restrictive that few eligible taxpayers took advantage of it.

A few years later, when the amount was increased and the rules were liberalized, more workers began participating. Still, the rules for self-employed individuals (and *their* employees) were nowhere near as generous as those covering people working for corporations. Legislation enacted during the 1980s provided virtual parity among corporate and self-employed workers, sharply reducing the use of Keogh plans as other options became available to sole proprietorships for covering their workers.

Within the corporate world itself, employees were not well protected before the mid-1970s. A litany of abuses by companies (and labor unions supposedly working in their members' behalf) finally led to passage of the Employee Retirement Income Security Act in 1974, the most comprehensive employee benefit legislation ever to come from Washington. Today, virtually every U.S. worker is protected by ERISA's sweeping provisions.

Among the safeguards this historic legislation now provides are strict rules on how and where pension money may be invested, provisions allowing workers to shift built-up benefits when they change jobs, and schedules for vesting (locking in the employer-contributed retirement benefits) of workers who remain with the same employer.

Buried within ERISA's voluminous text were provisions for the creation of individual retirement accounts. Like Keogh plans, the first IRAs provided limited deductions and carried strict eligibility requirements. A major deterrent to their immediate widespread use was the fact that they were available only to workers having access to no other retirement plan. It was not until changes in the law in 1981 made them available to all workers that the use of IRAs began to gain momentum.

While IRAs were broadened to allow workers to set up plans for their spouses, certain other provisions made them more limiting, a situation ameliorated somewhat by the availability of other options, which we discuss next. However, the so-called IRA rollovers also provided by ERISA have become widely used as parking places for retirement benefits distributed by a former employer when the employee leaves the job.

EMPLOYERS SHIFT RESPONSIBILITY TO WORKERS

During the 1980s, ERISA's strict rules governing the pension plans companies run for their employees led employers increasingly to shift away from these so-called *defined-benefit* plans, which committed them to future payments they might find difficulty in meeting. They opted instead for *defined-contribution* plans, which are funded largely through contributions made by employees themselves, and may or may not include employer contributions. Furthermore, any funds added by the company in a defined-contribution plan need not be cast in stone, allowing for flexibility that takes into consideration year-to-year swings in business fortunes.

These voluntary contributions from management include employee stock option plans (ESOPs), where instead of cash a corporation gives employees shares of its stock, which are placed in the employees' tax-qualified retirement plan accounts. Companies may also sponsor simplified employee plan IRAs (called SEP-IRAs) and salary reduction plan SEPs (SAR-

SEPs); and 401(k) or 403(b) plans,* to which they may, but are not obligated to, contribute.

To recap, enactment of the tax breaks for Keogh plans, trifling even by 1960s standards, came only after extended debate and considerable compromise. The provisions were subsequently liberalized. Later, ERISA provided the broad framework for the creation of retirement savings programs. Its provisions steered employers away from plans that required their funding and toward sponsorship of plans that allow their employees to determine the amount of their salary they want to put away for retirement and how they want the assets invested.

The pattern is unmistakable. We have a government that is, and will be, creating greater tax incentives for workers to save for their own retirement and providing more choices in the ways these workers may shelter their retirement savings from taxes. The trade-off will be a significant lowering of the benefits provided under Social Security and Medicare. Employers increasingly are opting for sponsorship of programs where workers must determine their own level of participation. Furthermore, this pattern is likely to continue. In addition, both the government and employers are shifting to employees the burden and responsibility of investing these funds wisely.

To give you an idea of how far we have progressed, by 1995, there were nearly a quarter million 401(k)s in operation, the fastest-growing type of retirement plan. The number of participants was approaching 20 million and total assets had exceeded half a trillion dollars.

The message is unambiguous: the government will provide the tax breaks and your employer will provide the means for

---

*These plans, named for the Internal Revenue Code sections that govern them, are similar; 401(k) plans are sponsored by companies and other for-profit organizations, while 403(b) plans are sponsored by certain not-for-profit entities such as educational institutions and charitable organizations.

you to take advantage of the tax breaks—*but it will be up to you to use these tax breaks and programs to build your own financial security.* Those who begin early and act wisely will be able to accumulate the wealth necessary for senior years that are financially secure; those who do not will have to rely on a "safety net" that may only provide a subsistence-level lifestyle in retirement—if indeed retirement will even be an option.

A LOOK AT YOUR CHOICES

For those of us who recall Washington's timid foray into retirement plan legislation three decades ago, what is available today is truly impressive. And, as I have said, it is only the beginning. Because change is an ongoing condition where these plans are concerned, you will have to make certain that the upcoming descriptions are current at the time you consider participation in any of them. I am providing the detail for you to use as a starting point and for purposes of comparison; your financial advisor can give you an update when you need it. Here are brief descriptions.

Individual Retirement Accounts

IRAs are for individuals looking for a tax-deferred savings plan. You may contribute 100 percent of your annual compensation to a $2,000 limit each year ($2,250 if you have a nonworking spouse). To be eligible, your contributions must come from earned income and you must be over age 18 and under age $70\frac{1}{2}$. You may set up and contribute to a plan for any year any time during the year and through April 15 of the following year. Earnings on plan assets are tax deferred and contributions may be tax deductible. Deductibility of contributions may be limited by participation in other plans and by your level of compensation. If you meet certain conditions, you may also place a certain amount of after-tax earned income in your IRA. It is important to note that under current law, you must begin taking distributions at age $70\frac{1}{2}$, either as a lump sum or at an annual rate based on your life expectancy or the life expectancy of you and your spouse. Failure to start making withdrawals by age $70\frac{1}{2}$ will result in a rather sharp penalty on top of income taxes owed.

IRA Rollovers

Proceeds from former employers' plans can be placed in IRA rollovers. Important note: keep an eye on the calendar. You have 60 days from the date you receive the distribution to open a rollover account and place these assets in it. If you do not, the proceeds will be subject to some stiff premature distribution penalties on top of the income tax that is due on them. Above all, do not yield to the temptation to spend these distributions. Besides the erosion that will occur from the payment of taxes and penalties, you will lose out on an opportunity to retain a significant amount in your wealth-building program and do perhaps irreparable damage to your future financial security.

Keogh Plans

These are available for small business owners and self-employed professionals. If you qualify, you can make tax-deductible contributions of up to 25 percent of your earned income each year, to a $30,000 limit (the maximum compensation on which contributions can be based is currently $150,000). The plan must be set up by December 31 to qualify for contributions that year. Earnings on contributions are tax deferred.

Simplified Employee Pensions

SEPs are attractive to smaller companies, including sole proprietors, partnerships, and subchapter S corporations seeking a plan with minimal annual administration, IRS filings, and paperwork. Up to 15 percent of an employee's compensation or $22,500, whichever is less, may be contributed to the plan each year. (The annual percentage limit for self-employed individuals is 13.043 percent.) The plan can exclude employees under age 21 and employees who have not worked for the employer in at least three of the past five calendar years. Employees who earned less than $400 can also be excluded. Employer contributions are discretionary. Contributions are tax deductible and 100 percent vested at all times. Earnings on plan assets are tax deferred.

Salary-reduction Plans

SAR-SEPs, variants of SEPs, are for companies with fewer than 25 employees seeking a simple retirement plan and wishing to offer salary-reduction features. Salary deferrals cannot exceed 15 percent of an employee's compensation or $9,240, whichever is less. The employee salary reduction and employer contribution together cannot exceed the lesser of 15 percent or $22,500 of an employee's compensation. Eligibility requirements are the same as those for SEPs, except that at least 50 percent of a company's eligible employees must elect to make salary deferrals in order for the company to sponsor a SAR-SEP. Company contributions are discretionary. Pretax employee contributions made through payroll deductions reduce the employee's current taxable income, and earnings on plan assets are tax deferred. All contributions are 100 percent vested at all times.

Profit-sharing Plans

These plans are designed for companies that wish to retain discretion over retirement plan contributions. Annual contributions may not exceed the lesser of 15 percent of an employee's compensation or $22,500 (for self-employed individuals, the rate is 13.04 percent). Participants must be at least 21 and/or have at least one year of service. A two-year eligibility period may be imposed if immediate vesting is provided. Employer contributions are discretionary and can be based on profitability. The maximum deductible contribution is 15 percent of an employee's compensation.

Money-purchase Plans

Companies willing to commit to an annual contribution and seeking a retirement plan that maximizes deductibility of employer contributions may find money-purchase plans attractive. Up to 25 percent of an employee's compensation or $30,000, whichever is less, may be contributed each year (20 percent if self-employed). Participants must be at least 21 and/or have one year of service. A two-year eligibility period may be imposed if immediate vesting is provided. Employer contributions are mandatory, at a rate set forth in the plan agreement.

401(k) Plans

These plans are for companies seeking a flexible, comprehensive retirement plan primarily funded by employees but also allowing for employer contributions. Annual contributions of up to 15 percent of an employee's compensation, to a $9,240 limit, are permitted; the employee salary reduction and employer contribution, however, cannot exceed the lesser of 15 percent or $22,500. Participants must be at least 21 and have at least one year of service. Employer contributions may be discretionary or mandatory, as set forth in the plan agreement. An employer may choose to match employee contributions and/or make discretionary profit-sharing contributions in addition to employee salary deferrals.

403(b) Plans

Individuals employed by not-for-profit organizations exempt under IRS Code 501(c)(3) and employees of public educational organizations can be covered by these plans. Annual contributions are allowed to the lesser of 20 percent of compensation or $9,500, subject to a maximum exclusion allowance based on years of service and compensation. Employer contributions can be made if the plan agreement provides for them. Pretax employee contributions are made through payroll deductions and reduce the employee's current taxable income. Earnings are tax deferred until they are distributed. Employee contributions are 100 percent vested at all times.

WHAT ABOUT ANNUITIES?

With life expectancies increasing and the future of Social Security in doubt, the risk of outliving retirement savings is growing. Couple this with the need to keep your capital growing faster than inflation, and you have powerful incentives for considering annuities as part of your investment plan. Strictly speaking, however, annuities are not retirement planning devices. Rather, they represent a cross between life insurance and savings/investment vehicles. They are attractive for a number of reasons. During the accumulation period, earnings on assets grow tax deferred, although, like tax-deferred retirement savings programs, they provide stiff penalties for withdrawal before age $59\frac{1}{2}$ in return for the privilege of allowing assets to build tax deferred. Annuities' protection feature safeguards beneficiaries against loss of principal and allows you to build an estate free of probate. During the payout period, they assure a steady flow of income for life or a stated number of years and can be set up to cover the lifetimes of one or two people, usually a husband and wife. Alternatively, you may take the built-up assets as a lump sum.

Assets in a *fixed annuity* grow at a predetermined rate that may be adjusted from time to time. Assets in the investment portion of a *variable annuity* fluctuate along with the market swings of the underlying securities. Most variable annuities, however, have a fixed option in which investors may place all or a portion of the annuity's assets. For some people, annuities represent the best of both worlds. They allow assets to grow tax deferred and they provide for a secure stream of income during the payout period. For other people, alternative investment vehicles offer more appeal.

How do you know whether you should include annuities in your financial plan? First of all, because of the premature distribution penalties, you probably should not invest in annuities if you will need the money before you retire. On the other hand, if you plan to set the money aside to build retirement capital for yourself, under current law in most states, you may leave assets in an annuity to continue building value until age 90 (85 in the others), as opposed to age $70\frac{1}{2}$, when you must begin withdrawing them from IRAs and other qualified retirement plans.

If you should choose to invest in an annuity and have several years to go before you retire, you may wish to consider a variable annuity rather than the fixed version. Like your other long-term investments, the assets in a fixed annuity simply will not grow fast enough to generate any meaningful wealth. Use a fixed annuity when your objectives are protection of your principal and assurance of a stated amount of income throughout the entire payout period.

In a variable annuity, you have a range of investment options, from conservative to more aggressive, and generally you will be able to shift your options as you pass various milestones in your life or your financial situation changes. Fees are another factor to consider carefully before choosing annuities over other investment vehicles. There are insurance fees to cover the guarantee of your principal, management fees to cover the cost of professional management, contract fees levied for the annual administration of the contract, and surrender fees, as well as the premature distribution penalties if you withdraw before age $59\frac{1}{2}$. As always, consult your financial advisor before you make a decision on whether an annuity is an appropriate investment vehicle for you.

SHIFT TAX BURDEN TO MINORS

Instead of setting assets aside for your minor children or grandchildren in an account under your control, consider opening accounts under the Uniform Transfers to Minors Act (UTMA) or Uniform Gifts to Minors Act (UGMA), depending on which law is applicable in your state. Every state and the District of Columbia has enacted such legislation, which allows any adult to contribute to a custodian account in a child's name without having to name a legal guardian or establish a trust. Each parent or grandparent can contribute up to $10,000 each year per child without incurring federal gift tax liability. In this way, the returns earned on your gifts become taxable at the minors' tax rates, rather than your own.

To illustrate the difference this tax savings can make in the accumulation of assets for the child, if you are subject to the 1995 maximum federal tax rate of 39.6 percent, the tax on a $1,300 return on assets would be $515. At 1995 rates, a child under 14 is allowed to receive up to $650 in unearned income tax free, since that is the amount covered by the child's standard deduction. The income between $650 and $1,300 is taxed at the child's rate, presumably 15 percent—or a tax of $98, less than one-fifth the amount of tax under your rate. I have already demonstrated what effect the power of compounding can have on such savings over time.

Almost any type of financial instrument is suitable for a custodian account. Thus, UGMA or UTMA accounts are more conducive to equity investments, which have historically provided the highest long-term returns. Custodian accounts also permit you to make contributions whenever you want, in whatever amount. This can be a great advantage, especially if you are putting money away for a child's education, because investing regularly will be the only way most people will be able to reach their goal, especially at tomorrow's projected college costs.

When setting up an UGMA or UTMA account, you must name a custodian. Most financial advisors say you should not name yourself, because the value of the account will be included in your estate if you die while the account is in existence. Instead, name your spouse, a family member, or a trusted friend.

Opening an account is easy and inexpensive. There are no special documents to prepare and no special tax returns to file as with a trust. All you need is the child's Social Security number and the signature of the custodian. Your financial advisor can help with the details.

THE BENEFITS OF INVESTING OFTEN

Regardless of your investment choice, you should add to your retirement fund as frequently as you can. In many cases, the decision is made for you in the form of payroll deductions. If it is not, seriously consider making arrangements to make your own contributions, such as systematic investment programs where withdrawals are automatically made from your checking or savings account. I would suggest that you do this monthly or twice monthly. The longer the interim between contributions, the less benefit you can derive from the dollar-cost averaging strategy we discussed in Chapter 6.

REMEMBER: PAPER GAINS
ARE NOT TAXED

Yet another excellent way to defer taxes is to invest in the common stocks of growth-oriented corporations—companies that pump most of their earnings back into building their businesses. As their businesses grow in value, the price of their stock rises. Holders of that stock will not have to settle up with the tax collector until they actually sell their shares. It is no wonder that these stocks are among the favorite investments of growth-oriented investors.

As we discussed in the previous chapter, a ready-made portfolio of such companies can be had by selecting an appropriate aggressive growth-stock mutual fund. Of course, there may be some capital gains taxes to pay each year as the fund's manager takes profits on portfolio trades, but these capital-gains distributions generally represent only a small proportion of the growth in the value of the shares. In any event, investors in these funds usually translate the distributions immediately into additional shares of the fund through automatic reinvestment programs. (However, you are obligated to pay the taxes on any income and gains distributions the fund makes in any year, even if the distributions are automatically reinvested for you.)

The main thing to keep in mind, however, is that the value added to your fund's shares through appreciation of the net asset value will go untaxed as long as you hold the shares. It is taxed only when you turn these paper gains into real gains by redeeming or exchanging shares. And, if you are investing for the long term, that eventuality may be many years in the future.

TAX AVOIDANCE: TAKING THE TAX COLLECTOR OUT OF THE LOOP

The best and most direct way to diminish the drag of taxes on your wealth-building efforts, of course, is to avoid taxes altogether. As I have said, achieving this objective has become increasingly difficult in recent years as Congress has closed loopholes and tightened the rules. While the options are limited for most people, there are still some things you can do. I should interject here that the rules and regulations covering taxation tend to be extremely fluid; details change from year to year, making it impractical to discuss specific points in anything but general terms.

The greater your after-tax income, the more will be available to fund your financial plan. The first place to look for ways to reduce your taxable income (to increase your after-tax income) is in the deductions you are allowed to take. It is neither illegal nor immoral to use the tax laws to the fullest extent possible in taking every allowable deduction. But to do so without over-stepping the bounds (and the bounds are becoming narrower and narrower), you must understand the rules and you must be able to back up any deductions that you do claim that might be challenged by the Internal Revenue Service. This means keeping good records. Pure guesswork is seldom a valid defense, though sometimes an educated guess is permissible, if it is reasonable. It is always a good idea to seek the help of your financial advisor when becoming involved with tax strategies.

If you own and operate your own business, no matter how small or how little of your time it might take, you can deduct costs directly related to that business. If you devote a portion of your home to the operation of the business, you may allocate to the business certain expenses incurred in running the house. If you purchase equipment used exclusively for the business, you may be able to depreciate the cost of the equipment. Likewise, if your work requires that you set aside a portion of your home as an office, you may deduct the expenses. I must caution you that these are areas in which the IRS in recent years has become much more strict. Be sure to keep your financial advisor fully informed.

If you own real estate from which you derive rental income, you may deduct all costs directly associated with the maintenance upkeep, and taxes, and you may take prorated deductions each year for depreciation.

Your advisor can also help you maximize deductions and minimize taxes on your investments. For example, you can use losses on one investment to offset gains on another, replacing both holdings with ones of greater quality. Or, if you wish to keep an investment on which you already have substantial gains, you can sell it and offset the gains against the losses on the investment you want to eliminate, then buy the favored investment back. This will allow you to raise your cost basis on the retained investment which, in turn, will confine future taxes to future gains.

If you use this maneuver, you must watch the calendar; the "wash sale" rule requires that in order to establish a loss, at least 30 days—either before or after the sale—must elapse before replacing the investment with a substantially identical one. Year-end maneuvers must be completed before the loss is established; and the loss must be taken in the year it is established. Again, your financial advisor can be of immense value in your tax planning.

DON'T OVERLOOK TAX-FREE MUNICIPAL BONDS

Once reserved only for the very rich, municipal bonds are increasingly being used by the general public to avoid taxation of income. Just because your income does not fall into the highest tax brackets, you should not overlook tax-free municipal bonds. Yields on these securities typically run around 80 percent of yields on U.S. Treasury bonds, and in the recent past they have exceeded 90 percent, in some cases running at parity with taxable bonds. This has made these securities extremely attractive to investors of moderate means. As Table 8.1 shows, it does not take a very high bracket to allow you to benefit from an investment in municipal bonds. When you consider that income from bonds issued by the state in which you live probably also escapes state income taxes, the potential benefit is even greater.

The only way to obtain a direct comparison between the performance of municipal bonds and that of fully taxable bonds is by comparing them on a taxable-equivalent basis. The table shows how much more a fully taxable investment must earn to

TABLE 8.1 The Tax-free Advantage

If a tax-free bond provides a yield of	Here is the taxable equivalent yield a fully taxable bond must provide at these tax rates				
	15%	28%	31%	36%	39.6%
3.0%	3.53	4.17	4.35	4.69	4.97
3.5	4.12	4.86	5.07	5.47	5.79
4.0	4.71	5.56	5.80	6.25	6.62
4.5	5.29	6.25	6.52	7.03	7.45
5.0	5.88	6.94	7.25	7.81	8.28
5.5	6.47	7.64	7.97	8.59	9.11
6.0	7.06	8.33	8.70	9.38	9.93
6.5	7.65	9.03	9.42	10.16	10.76
7.0	8.24	9.72	10.14	10.94	11.59
7.5	8.82	10.42	10.87	11.72	12.42
8.0	9.41	11.11	11.59	12.50	13.25

The taxable equivalent yield is calculated by dividing the tax-free yield by 1.00 minus the tax rate. Here is an example using a tax-free bond yielding 5% for an investor in the 39.6% tax bracket: 5 ÷ (1.00 − 0.396) = 8.28.

generate an equivalent tax-free yield at the various tax rates. As an example, for someone in a 36 percent federal tax bracket, an investment would have to earn 9.38 percent to match a 6 percent tax-free yield. Taxpayers in lower brackets can also benefit, but not to the same extent.

The table also reveals another important consideration. In judging performance, you must compare the tax-free return of a municipal bond investment with the after-tax return on a fully taxable investment. It is not what you earn that counts; it is what you keep. For example, over time, taxable investments, such as U.S. Treasury bonds, may appear to have better total returns than municipal bonds. However, when you compare the *tax-free* returns on municipal bonds with the *after-tax* return of Treasuries, municipals tend to outperform Treasuries on an after-tax basis.

PRACTICAL ALTERNATIVE: TAX-FREE MUTUAL FUNDS

For most of us, direct investment in municipal bonds is not practical. In the first place, the usual minimum denomination is $100,000. Unless you have plenty of money to invest, this does not allow for much diversification to protect your investment. In all likelihood, you also do not possess the required resources or expertise to keep close watch on the credit record and financial health of the issuers.

There is a very practical way, however, for you to invest in municipal bonds—tax-free bond funds. The following are some of the benefits these funds offer individuals who believe tax-free investments have a place in their financial program:

- *Availability.* Municipal bond issues generally are not available to the general public. They are offered first to large institutional investors and, as you would expect, the most attractive ones are quickly snapped up.
- *Instant diversification.* The moment you hold a single share of a tax-free bond fund, your investment is diversified among dozens of holdings. Shareholders of many municipal bond funds experienced the value of diversification firsthand when Orange County, California, defaulted on its bonds in late 1994. For them, the Orange County bankruptcy had a far lesser impact than for holders of a single Orange County bond.
- *Industry sector participation.* While municipal bond funds are not growth-oriented investments, they represent one way of investing in dynamic sectors of the economy. Many of these funds have holdings in such areas as the health care, housing, and waste management industries. Should the financial health of agencies within these sectors improve, existing bonds could increase in value. In addition, keep in mind that investing in these areas through

municipal bonds, as opposed to investing in equities or taxable bonds, is tax-free.

- *Professional management.* With a fund, you get the benefit of the expertise of a team of analysts who are constantly monitoring this trillion-dollar market in search of the most attractive debt. A bond fund's portfolio is constantly being updated, its securities being changed to take advantage of shifts in the market or opportunities that present themselves. The inability to reinvest proceeds from one holding into an equal or better investment is minimized because of the portfolio's diversification.
- *Liquidity.* It is much easier to purchase and redeem municipal bond mutual fund shares than to buy and sell individual bonds in the market.

Municipal bond funds also offer protection against these risks:

- *Interest-rate risk.* Diversification and active management of a fund's portfolio help soften the blow when interest rates fall. If you own one or even a handful of bonds, on the other hand, you are bearing the full impact of interest-rate risk.
- *Credit risk.* Orange County's difficulties highlight this type of risk. As a result of this situation, many individual Orange County bond issues were downgraded almost overnight—in some cases from AA to CCC by the bond rating services. While mutual funds cannot guarantee complete immunity from such precipitous events, their diversification may add a measure of protection.
- *Reinvestment risk.* With a municipal bond fund, you will be able to reinvest income and capital gains immediately in exactly the same vehicle. Finally, with a tax-free bond fund, you don't run the risk that you will not be able to reinvest proceeds from a maturing bond in a security with equal or better potential.

WILL TAX REFORM END
MUNICIPAL BOND TAX BREAKS?

The introduction of flat-tax proposals into the public discussion in early 1995 caused some concern among municipal bond investors. The proposals include those that would exempt from taxation the interest and dividends derived from all sources. Several points should be made as these proposals are aired in the media during the extended debate over tax reform that you can expect over the next several years.

If history is any guide, the U.S. government will be extremely reluctant to enact any tax law that would inhibit municipalities from attracting capital. The most likely outcome of any successful income-tax proposal, in my view, would be a low-rate progressive income tax structure with fewer tax brackets. Interest would still be taxable and dividends would be taxed just once—at the individual level.

Concerns over the possible effects of lower income tax rates on municipal bonds could be misplaced. Figure 8.2 shows why. In 1979–80, as tax reforms were the subject of a national debate, proposals included those calling for a considerable reduction in the existing tax rates, then at a 70 percent maximum. The concern was that municipal bond investors had purchased these bonds to avoid the high tax brackets of the 1970s, and that a lowering of the rates would have a detrimental effect on the prices of these securities.

The figure shows the maximum tax rates in effect between 1980 and 1995. During the 1980s, tax rates were indeed lowered, from 70 percent to 28 percent. On the same chart, we have plotted the performance of the Lehman Brothers Municipal Bond Index. As you can see, municipal bond prices soared during the 1980s. Someone coming down from Mars would be tempted to conclude from the chart that the best thing we could do for municipal bonds would be to lower tax rates.

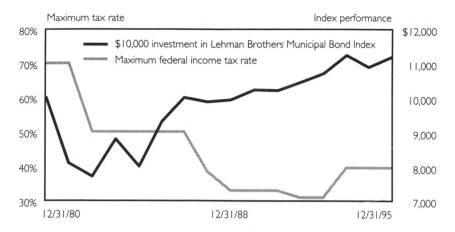

FIGURE 8.2 Despite the concern of many investors, the performance of municipal bonds did not suffer following the tax reductions of 1980. Chart compares performance of the Lehman Brothers Municipal Bond Index with the maximum federal income tax rate in effect during each period.

The reason municipal bonds did so well during the 1980s was that as a consequence of tax reform, interest rates dropped sharply during the period, more than offsetting the effects of declining tax rates. In my opinion, we will be facing a similar set of circumstances as tax reform once again becomes the subject of a great national debate. Tax reform, combined with spending restraint, should serve to address the nation's deficit problem appropriately. Combined with a low-inflation environment, the entire interest-rate structure could be reduced significantly over the next decade. Tax-free municipal bonds should continue to be attractive investments relative to the after-tax returns of taxable investments.

I should interject a note of caution here. As this national debate on taxes unfolds, concern over the possible effect on municipal bonds may keep the municipal bond market under a cloud. A realistic near-term expectation, therefore, would be that prices of tax-exempt securities may tend to underperform those of Treasury bonds. The spread between the yields of Treasury bonds and municipal bonds may narrow further, thus providing an excellent opportunity for taxpayers in all brackets to participate in this market.

DEFER TAXES—AT ANY RATE

Speaking of tax law changes, do not be misled into thinking that if rates actually come down significantly as the result of reform efforts, the benefits of tax deferral will no longer be worthwhile. That is definitely not the case; no matter how low your tax rate might drop, you will still be able to build more wealth by putting off taxes than you can by paying them as you go along. To be sure, the difference will not be as great, but it will be greater than it would be with all taxes paid before compounding. And, when building wealth, you must grab every advantage you can. Figure 8.3 illustrates the point by

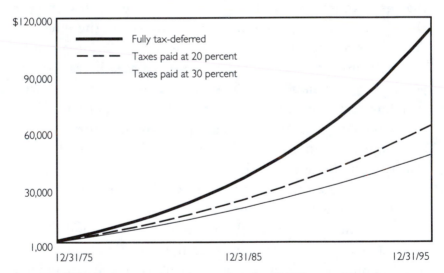

FIGURE 8.3 Chart compares the results of a $2,000 annual investment where taxes are fully deferred against $2,000 annual investments taxed at 20 percent and 30 percent, respectively, on which the income generated by the investment is also taxed.

comparing 20-year results of tax deferral with results at tax rates of 30 percent and 20 percent.

Since considerable time is likely to elapse before we have legislation that yields meaningful reduction in tax rates, this might be an appropriate place to suggest that while any time is a good time to make tax-deferred investments, the best time is when you can shift the tax burden from current high-tax dollars to dollars that are likely to be taxed at lower rates at some point in the future. Therefore, the appreciated value of income sheltered from today's relatively high tax rates will be further enhanced if it is taxed at significantly lower rates in the future.

DON'T OVERLOOK ESTATE AND INHERITANCE TAXES

While we are on the subject of taxes, it is important to mention estate and inheritance taxes. Although the federal estate tax rules were liberalized considerably in the 1970s, generally allowing estates of $600,000 or less to escape federal estate taxes, state inheritance taxes may kick in at much lower levels. These state levies, in fact, can be much more destructive to unprotected wealth than the federal tax.

Furthermore, in the years ahead, $600,000 will not seem like such a large estate. Inconceivable as you might find the idea today, individual net worths in excess of $1 million will be fairly commonplace in the not too distant future as people take more seriously the task of building their personal wealth. Therefore, as you begin to see your own assets grow, do not neglect to talk with your financial advisor about estate planning.

SO, WHAT SHOULD YOU DO NOW?

As you have undoubtedly noticed, the great majority of the tax-related information in this chapter has been tied to retirement planning. This should not surprise you. For the past 30 years, the federal government has been moving in the direction of offering the means for individual workers to take charge of their own affairs in terms of providing for a financially secure old age. The process will only accelerate as time goes on, as clearly indicated by the debate already under way in Washington and around the country.

Still, it will take many years to make the full transition from the present system of entitlements financed out of current tax revenues to one where workers put aside money for their own use in the future. And, most likely, it will never be a full transition, for there will always be that "safety net" for those most needy of it, whether they be workers who lacked the foresight or the resources to provide for themselves or those who encounter catastrophic expenses that only the most wealthy could manage alone.

The slow transition will ease the way for those who find themselves in mid-career having to address a whole new set of retirement-planning assumptions than those in place when they joined the workforce. Regardless of your present life stage, however, you must change your thinking at once and make the very most you can of your remaining years of work.

What messages, then, should you carry away from this chapter? Here are five:

1. *Save, save, save.* Take advantage of every break your employer and the government make available to you. If your employer provides profit sharing, place your share in a qualified retirement plan if it does not automatically go there under the employer's program. If your employer also sponsors a SEP-IRA, SAR-SEP, 401(k), or 403(b) plan, take advantage of that, as well. If you have resources left over after reaching the annual contribution limit, consider a variable annuity.

2. *Hide your savings from yourself.* Money you don't see is harder for you to spend. If you can contribute to any or all of the above retirement savings vehicles through automatic payroll deduction, do it. If not, arrange with your bank to send the monthly amount through an automatic withdrawal. If you can't do that, make sure the first check you write each month is one to your investment plan.

3. *Keep your investments working.* If you are holding retirement plan assets in a money-market fund because you can't decide where to invest it, sit down and make that decision. Get your financial advisor into the act to help you decide. Idle cash, like idle people, turns meager profit.

4. *Leave your holdings alone, but not untended.* Once you have made your investment decisions, do not continually second-guess them, and do not yield to any transient temptation to change them. Keep your eye on them, however, and make certain they are still fulfilling their mission in your financial plan. When they are not, or when your situation changes, then, and only then, make the appropriate changes.

5. *Keep your hands off your investments.* It is no accident that the government has imposed rather severe penalties on money withdrawn prematurely from tax-favored retirement plans. The tax breaks you enjoy have been granted to encourage you to provide for your future financial security. The stiff penalties are to help make sure that you do.

A final word: These plans the government is making available to you and any enhancements to them that are likely to come in the future are not for "someone else." They are for you. You must take the steps to use them. You must make the decisions on how to invest the assets in them. You must develop the discipline to contribute regularly to them and to resist any temptation to take money out of them.

NEXT: PUTTING IT ALL TOGETHER

The tax-qualified programs we have been discussing in detail in this chapter are but one part of your overall financial plan. They must be woven into a program that includes such long-term goals as purchasing and financing a home and providing for the education of children, as well as shorter-term objectives such as saving for a new automobile or vacation trips.

To be sure, you cannot possibly do all things at once, but neither should you put off one until you complete the other. In the next chapter, we will look at ways you can go about identifying all of your goals, prioritizing them, and working effectively toward them.

PART III

PUTTING IT ALL
TOGETHER

CHAPTER 9

BUILDING YOUR PLAN:
MOVE DECISIVELY,
BUT STAY FLEXIBLE

*"I am indeed rich, since my income is superior to my expense,
and my expense is equal to my wishes."*
—EDWARD GIBBON, *Memoirs*, 1814

A MESSAGE OF HOPE

The title of this book is *Independently Wealthy* for a reason.
Contrary to the impression it might give at first glance, the title is not intended to convey the idea that the book will tell you
what it takes to become a megamillionaire. (Although, if you
are young enough and apply the principles and techniques I
have provided, you should be able to gather assets well in excess of a million dollars during your working lifetime. Indeed,
young workers will find that they *must* build assets of that
magnitude to attain such independence in the coming economic
environment.) Rather, being independently wealthy means
having the ability to enjoy your retirement years free from reliance on your government, your family, and your friends for
financial support. Building this financial security in the new

economic era will require the creation of a substantial asset base during your working years.

In Chapters 1 through 4, we explored how we have arrived at our present place in history, why we are now at a crossroads, and what we can expect in the years ahead. Chapters 5 through 8 outlined the many alternative methods of building financial security. Now it is time to get into the specific ways in which you can achieve your own financial independence. At first, the task might seem daunting; so daunting, in fact, that you might be tempted to give up in despair. If so, you will have missed my message completely, for my intention in undertaking the writing of this book is to provide hope, to show you how you can take control of your own financial destiny in the coming age. This chapter may surprise you as to how attainable this goal is for most of us. So let's begin.

Establish Your Benchmarks

When you have selected a new physician and he or she has agreed to accept you as a patient, one of the first things that happens is the construction of your medical history. You will fill out a lot of forms and answer a lot of questions. You will be interviewed by the doctor or one of the members of the medical staff. Chances are, you will get a physical examination. Before your doctor can look after your physical well-being, he or she has to know something about you, your family, and your lifestyle—and what shape you are in right now.

A similar process takes place when you start working with your financial advisor. You will be asked to fill out forms and use work sheets. You may be asked to struggle through some questionnaires. You will be interviewed at length about your hopes, dreams, aspirations, expectations, and perceptions. Your finances will definitely get a thorough examination. But before helping you create a financial plan for yourself and your family, your advisor must have a good idea of who you are, where you are in your life and career, what your resources are now and are likely to be in the future. As I said in the chapter about selecting a financial advisor, you must be completely open and forthright during this process and throughout your relationship with your advisor. He or she cannot provide a solid working plan and ongoing counsel without complete information, up front and along the way.

As a starting point, your advisor will probably help you develop a "snapshot" of your present financial condition. This picture determines what is called your *net worth*—in short, how much more you own than you owe (see Table 1 in the Appendix). A yearly accounting of your net worth will give you an idea of how well you are progressing toward your goals and will help you to set your objectives for the next year. Suggestion: keep these annual statements; over time, they will become an excellent record of your family's financial progress.

Next, your advisor will help you supplement your net worth snapshot with a "moving picture" of your income and outflow over a specified period. Again, the starting point for creating your first *statement of operations* or *income statement*, as it is variously called, will be your current situation. (Table 2 that follows Table 1 in the Appendix provides an example.) You and your advisor will track your actual income and outgo over a recent time period, usually the past 12 months or the most recent full calendar year.

This exercise will give your advisor an idea not only of how much money you have to spend but how you and your family are actually spending it. If you are not already keeping track of your income and outgo, the information will probably be quite enlightening to you, as well. After analyzing this information, your financial advisor can show you how to build a budget for the year ahead. Again, by committing this statement of income and outgo to paper, you can see exactly where your money is going each year.

Once you can see where it is going, you will have a better chance of finding ways to free up cash to fund your various savings and investment programs. You can use last year's Income statement to help you draft next year's budget. And you can compare last year's income statement with last year's budget to see how close you came in projecting the cost of various budget items.

Before getting into the actual drafting of your budget, however, your advisor will carefully analyze your income statement. He or she will look for spending patterns that suggest ways you might be able to trim back, ways to reallocate funds more efficiently to avoid unnecessary expenditures, and ways to ease your tax burden to increase your after-tax income to provide more resources for your retirement plan.

Drafting Your Plan

Once you know how much you are worth, how you are spending your money, and how you will allocate next year's income, you and your financial advisor can turn to the bigger picture. In reviewing your total financial picture, your advisor will delve into such areas as making sure you and your family are adequately protected from loss through damage to property, loss of income through disability or death, and loss of wealth through huge medical bills or liability claims. Your advisor will also review the options available to you in protecting your wealth from estate and inheritance taxes.

However, since this book is primarily about helping you accumulate the wealth you will need to assure a financially secure future, I will leave detailed discussion of those other areas of your overall financial program to your advisor. We will confine our discussion here to such topics as determining realistic financial goals, setting your long-term and short-term objectives, reviewing your options in the pursuit of those goals and objectives, establishing your priorities, and putting your plan in writing.

Why put it in writing? First, by sitting down to write an actual document, you force yourself to think clearly, concisely, and rationally about what you need to do. Writing down your thoughts helps you identify the key issues you wish to address. It helps you organize your thoughts and crystallize your thinking. The written plan then serves as a reference document, or map, that you can consult from time to time to refresh your memory about what you have determined to be the course of your financial voyage and your time frame for reaching your goals.

It is something you can pull out from time to time to check your progress. You will find that, with a plan, it is easier to tolerate swings in the market value of your investments because you can refresh your memory as to your time horizon. Over time, you will then be able to see more clearly how little difference small and short-lived swings in the market actually make in the overall value of your holdings. Your plan thus becomes another form of discipline. Finally, your written plan serves as assurance that both you and your financial advisor fully understand and remember your goals and objectives and the course you have set for reaching them.

Begin drafting your plan by listing all the things you know you will need money for now and in the future. The basics, of course: food, heat, light, shelter, clothes, transportation, and emergency fund; intermediate-term items such as a new car, a family vacation, and orthodontics; and, finally, longer-term (and much bigger-ticket) items such as saving for (and financing) a home, education for the children, possible care of aging parents, and maybe the biggest item of all, providing for your own retirement.

A Tall Order—but Not Necessarily an Impossible One

"Wow," you might be saying at this point. "Am I going to be able to do all of this? And if I am, how will I do it?" As I have already discussed, it will not be easy, and it will take knowledge and discipline. But I will also give you some good news, whether you are young, middle-aged, or older. Your task is "do-able." Think about some daunting challenge you have faced—and overcome—in your life. It might have been cleaning out the cellar or garage as a youth. It might have been managing a huge and complicated project at work. It might have been writing a book (tell me about it!). How did you face the challenge and win? By drafting a good plan, then taking one step at a time. One sweep of the broom. One hour on the computer. One word on paper. Then the next and the next, until the task was completed.

The same philosophy can be applied to meeting your major financial challenges. The process of writing your financial plan will force you to state clearly your long-, intermediate-, and short-term financial goals and objectives. In your plan, you will order your financial priorities, determine the financial vehicles to use, and set a timetable for achieving them.

The more years you have to build wealth, of course, the easier the task will be. Conversely, the longer you wait, the more risk you will have to take or the more cash you will have to commit to attain the goals you might have reached more safely and economically with an earlier start.

"Easy for you to say," you might be thinking if you are an older worker who predicated your entire retirement income planning on the prospect of Social Security and Medicare continuing at their present levels indefinitely, and built your own assets accordingly. I said there is a brighter side to the story, and I had you in mind, as well as the younger workers who still have many years in which to build their assets.

I said it did not matter at what age you begin an investment program, but that the important thing is to start it now. The main reason is simply that it is better to start late than not to start at all. But another reason in this case has to do with the new economic philosophy I have been writing about in this book. The changes I have discussed will take some time to implement fully. The process will not occur overnight. Entitlements such as Social Security and Medicare will not disappear in the blink of an eye. Their benefits may stop growing as rapidly each year as they have in the past, but they will not suddenly be yanked from beneath workers who designed their lives around the expectation that these benefits would be there for them.

But even if they do not disappear outright in the years to come, these entitlements will undergo major reductions in the not-too-distant future, I am convinced of that. It will not be by chance that the greatest impact of these changes will fall upon those who have only recently begun their careers; the government will implement these changes at a pace that will give everyone, regardless of age, time to adjust to them.

Older workers, who have the least time to make major adjustments to their financial plans, will still enjoy the fullest benefit of Social Security and Medicare. Middle-aged workers will face a greater impact, and even if they have done little up to this point in preparation for retirement, they still have time to shift their financial courses. Those with 20 or more working years ahead of them are just entering their highest earning phase and, in many cases, their heaviest financial burdens, such as buying homes and paying for college educations, are behind them. They are, therefore, in a position to commit a greater portion of their income to building assets for retirement.

Younger workers—all too often the ones for whom retirement planning seems like a distant problem—face massive changes in government welfare and entitlement programs. For this age group, the coming changes will require major adjustments both in outlook and in the allocation of the income they are earning now and will earn in the future. What is imperative is that this group recognizes the full impact of these coming changes now and makes the proper course corrections immediately.

There is yet one more option for those who need to accumulate more resources in order to retire comfortably. It is found in the longevity tables: these individuals can continue working.

With a greater proportion of the population now living beyond the arbitrary retirement age of 65 established by Frederick the Great for his career soldiers, many of us not only will be able, but will be eager, to stay on the job. If you are among those who have delayed building for retirement, you may also be delaying retirement, as well.

One sure way for the government to foster self-reliance would be to allow workers to stay on the job longer. Federal and state laws may be amended to permit workers to extend their productive years well beyond the current retirement age. That prospect need not necessarily be anticipated negatively, especially if you expect to be in good health when you reach the conventional retirement age. You may wish to remain on your present job, or you may take that as a time to try something different. Remember, many exciting and profitable ventures have been launched by those in their senior years.

BUILDING YOUR INVESTMENT PROGRAM

Once you know where you are going and how you can get there, you can begin putting your plan into action. You will have to make some choices, because you cannot hope to achieve all of your goals and objectives at once. Nevertheless, you should not put off the move toward one objective just because you have not yet attained an earlier one. While you may not be able to realize all of your goals and objectives at once, you can at least start working toward the largest and most distant of them at once. In fact, not only *can* you do this; you *must* do it if you hope to meet your goal.

LIFE-STAGE INVESTING

In a moment we will discuss some investment options and some suggested ways you can build your portfolio. I will provide some illustrative strategies and techniques you can use to help you build assets. I will also recommend some tools you can use to help you determine how much you will need for a comfortable retirement, and how much you will be required to save along the way to build the asset base you will need. But first, let us consider in general terms how your long-term assets should be allocated, depending on where you are in your life stage.

As we move through life, our investment needs change. As these needs change, so does the way we allocate our assets. Here are some basic rules for setting up and maintaining an investment program and some examples of how you might allocate your assets at your current life stage. These examples should be considered only as guidelines; you and your financial advisor may have good reasons for structuring your investment program differently.

1. *Determine your investment goals and objectives.* Objectives, as we have discussed, may include a new car, a boat, a home, or college education expenses. These objectives typically improve your lifestyle and are usually accomplished during your working years. Goals, on the other hand, are typically longer term in their nature, such as building financial security in retirement, and their funding usually spans your entire working years. One important caveat: be sure your goals and objectives are realistic, a determination that only you can make.

2. *Evaluate your risk tolerance.* Generally, risk tolerance is higher for younger investors with longer timelines and lower for older investors who may depend on their investment program for current income.

3. *Allocate your investable assets appropriately.* Your financial advisor will help you determine how much of your investable dollars should be allocated to each investment category: growth, growth-and-income, income, and tax-advantaged. If your investments are within the same mu-

tual fund company, you can adjust your allocation quickly and easily as your financial needs change—by shifting assets from one fund to another within the fund family, usually without incurring a service fee or other costs. Figure 9.1 provides four examples of how you might allocate your investment assets, depending upon your age and life stage.

You will notice that even the most aggressive growth-oriented portfolio includes some growth-and-income investments and some income investments. These investments tend to bring diversification to the program. In most cases income-oriented stocks are those of more mature, hence more conservative, companies. Or, the income-producing securities in the portfolio are fixed-income investments that trade on the bond market, which generally moves differently from the stock market. Either way, their presence in the portfolio is designed to help moderate the effects of a sharp decline in the stock market. The more aggressive the portfolio, the less reliance there will need to be on such investment vehicles.

The two middle portfolios, are subtly but distinctly different. One, geared for growth with some income, is for workers who are at the midpoint of their careers and still focusing essentially on growth of assets. The other, for investors approaching retirement and geared for income with some growth, represents the start of the transition of the portfolio toward the income that soon will be needed in retirement. Both are also designed to benefit from diversification.

The closer you are toward reaching your goal, the more conservative your strategy should become. You will notice, however, that even in the example for older investors (the most conservative of the allocation strategies) some assets are committed to growth-type investments. The main reason for this is that, regardless of your age, at retirement, you will have to consider the effects of inflation on the income your assets gen-

SEEKING MAXIMUM GROWTH

Risk tolerance: Generally investors with a higher risk tolerance (often in their 20s and early 30s).

40%–50%	Growth
30%–40%	Growth and income
5%–20%	Income or tax-free income

SEEKING GROWTH AND SOME INCOME

Risk tolerance: Generally investors with a high to moderate risk tolerance (often in their late 30s and early 40s).

30%–40%	Growth
40%–50%	Growth and income
10%–30%	Income or tax-free income

SEEKING INCOME AND SOME GROWTH WITH PROTECTION AGAINST INFLATION

Risk tolerance: Generally investors with a moderate risk tolerance (often in their late 40s and 50s).

10%–20%	Growth
30%–40%	Growth and income
25%–60%	Income or tax-free income

SEEKING HIGH CURRENT INCOME AND PROTECTION AGAINST INFLATION

Risk tolerance: Generally investors with a moderate to low risk tolerance (often over 60 and retired).

20%–30%	Growth
30%–40%	Growth and income
40%–70%	Income or tax-free income

FIGURE 9.1 These sample portfolios suggest some ways you might diversify your portfolio, depending upon your investment objectives and risk tolerance.

erate. Equity-type growth investments, as we have shown, provide the best potential for generating returns well in excess of inflation.

SOME REAL-LIFE EXAMPLES

While hypothetical examples can and do serve a purpose, it is important to see how this works in the real world. Let's take a look at how some mutual funds have actually performed. I will use Putnam funds because these are the ones with which I am most familiar, though there are many other mutual funds with excellent records that would manifest similar results (be sure to consult the prospectus of any fund before you invest). While past performance should never be taken as a guarantee of future results, these examples can serve as a guide for the kind of performance a certain type of fund is likely to experience.

To illustrate the point, Figure 9.2 shows the results of a $1,000 investment in an aggressive growth fund (Putnam Voyager Fund) and a fund that invests in both growth and income stocks and bonds (The Putnam Fund for Growth and Income) over the 25 years ended December 31, 1995. For purposes of comparison, I have also included the performance of the Standard & Poor's 500 Stock Index, a widely accepted measure of stock market performance, and the Consumer Price Index, which will show inflation over the period. Results assume reinvestment of all distributions. The funds' results are shown after deducting the maximum sales charge, but those for the indexes do not take into account any fees or commissions.

The difference in the performance of these two funds during the period reflects the differences in their objectives, a subject we discussed in Chapter 7. Putnam Voyager Fund is an aggressive growth fund that focuses on maximizing capital apprecia-

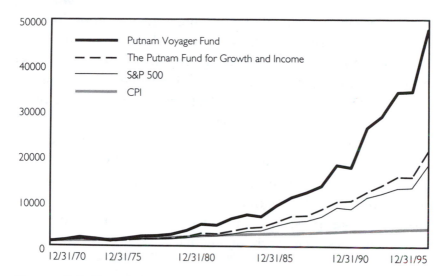

FIGURE 9.2 Chart compares the cumulative 25-year performance of an aggressive growth fund (Putnam Voyager Fund), a fund whose portfolio consists of both stocks and bonds (The Putnam Fund for Growth and Income), the stock market at large (S&P 500 Index), and inflation (the Consumer Price Index).

tion and generates virtually no current income. Its annual distributions consist mainly of capital gains generated by the sale of securities that have grown in value since being added to the portfolio. The Putnam Fund for Growth and Income seeks both capital growth and some current income and invests in both stocks and bonds. Hence, it tends to be the more conservative of the two funds.

SOME USEFUL TOOLS FOR MAINTAINING DISCIPLINE

In an earlier chapter, we discussed some of the strategies you can use to make sure you contribute regularly to your investment program. As a reminder and quick review, here they are again. Pay yourself first; make sure the first check you write each month is the one for your investments. Make the process even easier by setting up a systematic investment plan; instruct your bank to forward a prescribed amount automatically to your investment plan every month.

Still better, if you can arrange it, make your payment through payroll deduction where you work. Did you ever wonder why the government instituted tax withholding? The reason is simple: the government gets the money before you spend it. Take a lesson from the government by instituting your own investment-withholding plan.

REVIEW YOUR PLAN PERIODICALLY

At this point, we should talk about the need to review your financial plan and your investment program from time to time. The written plan is intended as a semipermanent document, one that should be drafted carefully at the outset to serve as a general guide and one that should not need to be constantly revised. Nevertheless, you should not consider it to be something that is cast in stone. Even the Constitution of the United States, one of the most permanent sets of rules in human history, has been amended several times. In fact, if you recall your American history, the ink was barely dry on the final draft when the Founding Fathers added 10 amendments known as the Bill of Rights. Changes in the business and investment climate, the fortunes of the companies in which you have invested, or your own personal or family circumstances, may call for you to make changes in your investment program from time to time.

If circumstances require changes in your financial plan or in your investment program, by all means make them. But you should do so only after deliberate thought and consultation. To make sure your program is still valid, however, you should review it periodically. How often? That is up to you, but I am reminded of the woman who had a strawberry patch that she was eager to grow larger and make more productive. So anxious was she about the well-being of her strawberry plants that she dug them up every day to check their roots. Can you imagine how much help that was to the plants? How much faster do you think your investments will grow if you check on their prices every day in the paper? It is not necessary to review your program too often. Two or three times a year would certainly seem adequate. But I suggest a minimum of once a year, maybe around tax time so you are focusing on these important financial, investment, and tax issues at the same time.

HOW MUCH WILL YOU NEED FOR A COMFORTABLE RETIREMENT?

Many retirement planning specialists suggest that you should have enough assets to generate 80 percent of what you were earning at the time of retirement. Of course, you can use a larger or smaller percentage depending on how active you think you will be when you retire. Remember, the closer you are to retirement age now, the more likely it is that government supplements like Social Security and Medicare will still be available to you.

If you are several years or even decades away from retirement, making such projections with precision becomes difficult. The best you can hope to do is to make an educated guess. The biggest imponderable is inflation. While inflation is well under control now, it ran rampant in the 1970s, throwing all kinds of calculations to the wind. One of the great benefits of the new economic philosophy and the constraints the market has placed on policymakers is the prospect for inflation to remain modest for years to come. Since 1990, the inflation rate has remained below 3 percent. For planning purposes, a 3 percent to 4 percent inflation assumption seems realistic in the new economic era.

That said, the first step in making your projections is to estimate your annual income at retirement. Suppose a worker is
now 30 years old and earning $30,000 a year. If the worker
plans to retire in 35 years and expects to receive more than
cost-of-living salary increases over the years, let us say 4 percent on average (3 percent inflation, plus 1 percent merit),
when the worker reaches age 65, using those assumptions, he
or she would be earning about $113,000 a year.

Next, suppose the worker wants to retire at 100 percent of
the income in the final year of work. I chose 100 percent because I believe most Americans would consider themselves independently wealthy if they could retire on 100 percent of
their final year's income. How large would the asset base have
to be to produce that amount in the first year of retirement? To
achieve this income level, and assuming invested assets would
produce an annual return of 9 percent, the worker would need
assets of $1.26 million at retirement.

How Much Will You Need to Invest to Reach Your Goal?

Before you throw in the towel and say, "It can't be done!" let's
look at the arithmetic. The following illustration uses the actual results achieved by one of the mutual fund industry's old-
est funds, The Putnam Fund for Growth and Income. If, starting January 1, 1960, our 30-year-old worker had invested 5.5
percent of each year's salary over the 35-year period ended December 31, 1995, he or she would have accumulated $1.32 mil-
lion. This total resulted from an average annual growth rate of
12.6 percent and came in above the $1.26 million needed to
generate a return of $113,000 to match the salary during the
final year of work. As with the other examples, it takes into account the initial sales charge and assumes reinvestment of all
distributions.

While past performance of any mutual fund cannot be taken
as assurance of future results, this illustration suggests that,

under rather reasonable assumptions, the goal of accumulating a capital base adequate for providing financial security in retirement is a realistic expectation.

Because this example applies to a 30-year-old, it may be easy for you to get discouraged if you are older and have yet to begin saving for retirement. Do not lose heart. Sometimes real life can be more exciting (and rewarding) than fiction. You see, when the actual performance of an investment program is used, as in our example, becoming independently wealthy, even when you begin your investment program in middle age, is achievable and within your grasp.

Furthermore, no matter at what age you start investing for retirement, the task may not be as staggering as it sounds. There is a good chance that you are already building up some retirement assets through a pension or profit-sharing plan where you work. While that plan might not be generous enough or invested aggressively enough to provide all of the assets you will need to retire comfortably, chances are it is a significant beginning. With the help of your financial advisor, you might be able to invest some of the assets you have already accumulated more efficiently and effectively.

Therefore, when you begin making your projections, your concern will be in filling the gap between what your employer's plan will provide and what you will need to continue to enjoy your present standard of living. You can use the work sheet in Table 3 in the Appendix to come up with a rough approximation of the size of the gap and what it would take to fill it.

Using the same assumptions we used for the 30-year-old investor, a worker who waited until age 40 to begin investing for retirement would be earning $44,408 and would have to save 10 percent of each year's salary over the next 25 years to meet the $1.26 million goal at retirement.

A worker at age 45, with a salary of $54,029, could also meet the goal by setting aside 10 percent of salary for investment each year—if he or she had already accumulated $27,000 from other sources. Such an assumption is not at all unrealistic. After all, as I have said, the worker had probably been in the workforce for more than two decades and might well have been able to build assets through retirement plans and other savings.

Clearly, all of these projections are sensitive to the assumptions I am making here. If the worker chooses a higher or lower inflation rate, a higher or lower wage rate, or a higher or a lower return on assets, the changed assumptions will affect the results. Your financial advisor can help you determine the appropriate assumptions for your circumstances.

HOW LONG WILL YOUR ASSETS LAST?

There is yet another consideration. Suppose the worker expects to spend 20 years in retirement. Prices are not going to stop rising just because he or she is no longer working. The $113,000 annual income at retirement would also have to rise by 3 percent each year, using the same inflation assumptions we used during the accumulation period. By the time the worker is 85 years old, he or she would need to be receiving about $208,000 a year to maintain the same standard of living during retirement.

Now, suppose the worker had retired and started a withdrawal plan at age 65, taking out 9 percent of the $1.26 million in accumulated assets to make up the $113,000 in first-year retirement income. Assuming 3 percent annual increases in the amount withdrawn to account for inflation, and the same 12.6 percent annual average growth rate of The Putnam Fund for Growth and Income during the accumulation period, assets would last 24 years, and in the twenty-fourth year, the investor, at age 89, would be taking out $223,015. Alternatively, at growth rates of 8 percent and 9 percent, the assets would last 17 years and 20 years, respectively.

How long will *your* money last? Naturally, if your assets grow faster than you draw them out, your capital will last indefinitely. However, if you must draw out a bit of capital each time you make a withdrawal, you will eventually consume all of your assets. You can use Table 4 in the Appendix to come up with a rough estimate of how fast you can draw out assets before they are gone. To use the table, find the column showing the percentage at which you expect assets to grow in the Growth Rate line. Then determine the percentage you expect to draw each year from assets in the Withdrawal Rate column. The number where the Growth Rate column and the Withdrawal Rate line intersect represents the approximate number of years your assets will last.

Keep in mind that the number of years shown in the table is only an estimate and it does not take into account the effects of inflation. However, many mutual fund companies can provide you with hypothetical illustrations that will show you how long your assets will last under various assumptions. All you and your advisor need to do is supply the relevant information.

Preparing to Set Sail

By using the information you find in this chapter, and with the help of your advisor and the work sheets in the Appendix, you will be able to put together your own financial and investment program. Then, in the final chapter, you will find a set of rules that encapsulates the key points I have sought to make in this book—rules that should serve as a guide to help you to build the assets you will need to make you independently wealthy as the term is defined in this book.

CHAPTER 10

Summing Up: Ten Rules That Can Make You Independently Wealthy

"First say to yourself what you would be; and then do what you have to do."

—Epictetus, *Discourses*, Book 3, transcribed c. 150 A.D.

As discussed earlier, the greatest problem most of us face in the new economic era is building financial security. In the course of this discussion, I have also given you the good news that the emerging environment will be conducive to solving this problem. But you must take your financial destiny into your own hands, and the following rules may serve as a guide to that end.

1. Start Now

It is time, not timing, that makes compounding work best. The earlier you initiate your investment program, the longer your money can work for you. Don't let anyone discourage you from starting your plan by telling you it is too late. The only one who can prevent you from achieving your goal is you—by procrastination and inertia.

2. SET REALISTIC GOALS AND OBJECTIVES

Be realistic in setting your goals and objectives—this often means setting them *high* enough. One of the most important reasons for writing this book has been to point out that becoming independently wealthy *is* a realistic goal, and to show you how such a goal can be within your grasp.

3. CHOOSE A COMPETENT ADVISOR

A successful voyage depends upon a skilled navigator. Choose your financial advisor as carefully as you choose your investments, for this is one of the most important investments you will make. The ABCs of selecting an advisor are: accessibility, believability, and compatibility. Once you have made your choice and feel comfortable with it, you must provide your advisor with full disclosure, up front and on a continuing basis. The advice you receive can be only as good as the information on which it is based.

4. EDUCATE YOURSELF

Knowledge is power. The more familiar you are with the various aspects of financial and investment planning, the more knowledgeable you will be when speaking with your advisor. Here are some good ways to keep up.

- *Seminars.* Your financial advisor probably knows of investor-oriented meetings, seminars, and information sessions, and might well sponsor them from time to time. Your employer might also hold sessions relating to the company's programs covering retirement, health care, and other benefits. Since these programs can represent 25 percent or more of your total compensation, they have a major bearing on your financial security. Attend as many such sessions as you can.

- *Periodicals and newsletters.* Your local library may subscribe to a number of such publications. Do some browsing. If you find a few that capture your interest, drop in from time to time and read them. Some examples include newsletters such as *Kiplinger's Washington Letter*, newspapers including *The Wall Street Journal*, *Barron's*, *Investor's Business Daily*, and the *Financial Times* of London, and magazines such as *Money*, *Smart Money*, and *Kiplinger's Personal Finance Magazine*. But do not consider the articles as investment advice, regardless of how they are presented. Changes in your financial plan should only be made after thorough consultation with your advisor.

- *The information highway.* If you have access to the Internet, you may be able to do some productive surfing. One by one, the major mutual fund organizations are inserting their own Web pages on the World Wide Web. Many have even begun placing fund prospectuses on their Web pages and providing information about how to place direct orders for opening accounts and purchasing shares.

5. Pay Yourself First

Invest your money before you spend it. Treat your investment program as another necessity, along with food, shelter, transportation, and recreation. Write the check to your investment program first. Whenever possible, utilize systematic investment programs that make investments automatically for you by deductions from your checking or savings account. Alternatively, arrange for payroll deductions to finance your investments, if you can.

6. INVEST REGULARLY

Understand and take advantage of the concept of dollar-cost averaging. Once you begin such a program, maintain discipline by forcing yourself to keep up with it. Investing should become a habit. Make your investments as frequently as practicable. Monthly or semimonthly payments are more effective over time than those made quarterly, semiannually, or annually.

7. CHOOSE YOUR INVESTMENTS CAREFULLY

Always make sure your investments match your objectives. If you are seeking long-term capital appreciation, select growth-oriented investments. If you are seeking current income, select investments that are designed to provide it. Choose investments that are consistent with your tolerance for risk. Set realistic expectations for your investments. Remember, slow and steady carries the day. Don't swing for the seats; baseball games are won with lots of singles and doubles. If you swing for seats, you may find that you strike out as many times as you score. And don't swing at every pitch. Some of your best investment decisions will be the "opportunities" you passed up.

8. DIVERSIFY

Remember these time-tested maxims: Spread your risks. Don't put all your eggs in one basket. Invest in several companies. If one falters, the loss may be minimized by the positive performance of others. Invest in well-diversified companies representing several industries. Look for companies that are succeeding in a variety of businesses. Along the same lines, diversification among several industries should minimize the negative effect if one industry goes into a cyclical decline. Diversification can serve to reduce the volatility of your portfolio.

Spread your assets among several different mutual funds. Perhaps consider investing in more than one mutual fund management company. This may enable you to take advantage of different management styles. International diversification of assets can enable you to participate in an expanding world economy.

9. BE AN OWNER, NOT A LENDER

Wealth is built by those who own a portion of the economic machine and who are willing to undertake a degree of risk in the process of accumulating assets. For most of us, ownership is achieved through equity investments such as common stocks and mutual funds that focus on these securities.

Wealth is rarely achieved by those who choose only to lend their money—to banks in the form of savings accounts and to corporations and the government through bonds and other fixed-income securities. No matter where you are in your life cycle, some degree of ownership and risk-taking is essential. What is important is that you manage these risks intelligently.

10. AVOID TEMPTATION

If you are investing for a long-term goal, do not be tempted to spend those assets on a short-term purpose. Consider funds for shorter-term objectives and emergencies separately. If you receive a large distribution from a retirement plan as the result of a job change, place it *immediately* in an IRA rollover. Yielding to the temptation to spend some or all of this money can have an even more devastating effect on your long-term financial security than the taxes and heavy penalties imposed on premature distributions.

COPY AND REVIEW OFTEN

So here you have 10 rules that can help you build the wealth you will need to assure your future financial security.

1. Start now.
2. Set realistic goals and objectives.
3. Choose a competent advisor.
4. Educate yourself.
5. Pay yourself first.
6. Invest regularly.
7. Choose your investments carefully.
8. Diversify.
9. Be an owner, not a lender.
10. Avoid temptation.

YOUR FINANCIAL DESTINY: CHANCE OR CHOICE?

We have covered a lot of ground in this book. We have discussed the workings of the country's political and economic systems, the markets, investment vehicles, and more. But, in sum, this book has been about choice. *Your* choice. Your retirement should be the reward for hard work, not a punishment for becoming older. In this regard, it is my firm belief and conviction that none of us has to leave his or her financial future to chance. Our financial destiny is up to us. What it really takes to become financially secure in this new economic era is knowledge, discipline, and determination.

You may have started reading this book feeling alone, confused, and abandoned at sea. But now you have your charts and compass in hand, and you have learned how to locate your navigator. As the captain of your vessel, you are ready to set sail confidently on your journey to financial security. Bon voyage!

Appendix

Financial Planning Work Sheets

The work sheets on the following pages are provided to help you plot your course toward financial independence. The results you obtain from these work sheets are intended to serve only as estimates and should not be taken as financial advice. The personal information you use to complete them most likely will change with time. Your financial advisor can help you obtain more accurate results and determine if they are appropriate for your situation.

TABLE 1 Sample Net Worth Work Sheet

As of _____ ____, 19___

Assets		Liabilities	
Cash on hand (including savings and checking accounts, etc.)	$_____	Outstanding balance on home mortgage	$_____
Cash value of life insurance policies	_____	Outstanding balance on home equity loans	_____
Cash value of retirement program (usually money you have contributed or in which you have a "vested" interest)	_____	Outstanding property taxes	_____
		Outstanding balance on auto loan or lease	_____
Market value of your home	_____	Outstanding balance on credit cards and installment loans (if more than one month old)	_____
Market value of other real property (vacation home, land, etc.)	_____	Outstanding loans against life insurance policies	_____
Current value of home furnishings	_____	Outstanding medical and dental bills	_____
Current value of other personal belongings	_____	Other bills more than one month old	_____
Current market value (or turn-in value) of automobiles	_____	Other debts or obligations	_____
Current market value of securities (including current redemption value of U.S. Savings Bonds)	_____		
Current value of other assets	_____		
Total assets	$_____	Total liabilities	$_____

Total assets $_____ less total liabilities $_____
equals your net worth: $_____

TABLE 2 Sample Income Statement Work Sheet

For 12 months ended _____ ____, 19____

Income		Outgo	
Gross earned income from:		Investment program (pay yourself first!)	$_____
First spouse's salary, wages, and other job-related sources (bonuses, commissions, etc.)	$_____	Total costs for shelter:	
		Mortgage or rent	_____
		Heat	_____
Second spouse's salary, wages, and other job-related sources (bonuses, commissions, etc.)	_____	Electricity	_____
		Water	_____
		Sewer	_____
		Real estate taxes	_____
Other work	_____	Repairs and upkeep (itemize and specify below)	_____
Gross income from rental property	_____	Food:	
		Groceries, etc.	_____
		Meals out	_____
Gross unearned income from:		Clothing	_____
		Health and medical (in excess of insured coverage):	
Savings accounts (including certificates of deposit)	_____	Medical	_____
		Dental	_____
Dividends and other distributions from securities and other investments	_____	Prescriptions	_____
		Insurance:	
		Homeowners	_____
		Automobile	_____
		Health/Medical	_____
		Umbrella liability	_____
Gross income from all other sources	_____	Recreation:	
		Entertainment	_____
		Vacations	_____
		Other expenditures	_____
Total income	$_____	Total expenditures	$_____

TABLE 3 Retirement Planning Work Sheet

Step 1: How Much Will You Need at Retirement?

As you will recall, in my examples in the text I have used 100 percent of your income at retirement as a goal you should consider setting for yourself. This level of income would enable you to enjoy a lifestyle in retirement that equals the lifestyle you enjoyed while you were working. To use this goal as your starting point, begin your retirement planning exercise by writing in your current income where indicated below.

$_____

[A] You and/or your spouse's total
current income in today's dollars

The Social Security Administration recommends that the average retired person have enough money saved to generate 80 percent of what he or she was earning at the time of retirement. If you wish to use this as your goal, enter the information below and complete the calculation.

$_____   × .80 = $_____

You and/or your   [B] Required income
spouse's total current   in today's dollars
income in today's dollars
(from A)

TABLE 3 Retirement Planning Work Sheet (*Continued*)

Next, see how much you would receive in Social Security benefits if you were eligible today.

Determine your annual benefit from the 1995 Social Security Table below. Then, enter any other sources of regular income or benefits, such as survivor or disability benefits, you and/or your spouse either have now or expect to have when you retire.

$_____* + $_____ = $_____

Social Security   Other sources   [C] Total annual benefits

*If you are 45 or younger, enter "0"; consider any Social Security benefits you ultimately receive as a "bonus."

I. 1995 SOCIAL SECURITY FULL ANNUAL BENEFITS

Current gross income	$12,000	$20,000	$30,000	$44,000	$61,200+
Individual benefit	6,480	8,868	11,820	13,476	14,388
Individual and spouse benefit	9,720	13,296	17,724	20,208	21,576

The figure in the table under your current annual gross income is the approximate benefit you would receive if you were to retire today.

Social Security provides only a base level of income. The age at which full benefits begin is currently 65. The earliest you can receive retirement benefits is age 62, but the amount would be permanently reduced by 20% from the benefits paid at age 65. Starting in the year 2000, the normal retirement age will be increased in monthly steps until it becomes 67 in 2027. The federal government adjusts benefit payments to compensate for inflation. These work sheets adjust for inflation at an annual rate of 4%.

TABLE 3 Retirement Planning Work Sheet (*Continued*)

Now subtract your total annual benefits from your required income in today's dollars.

$_____   –   \$_____   =   \$_____

| Total current income (from A) or required income (from B) in today's dollars | Total annual bene- fits you will receive (from C) | [D] Retirement income you will need in today's dollars |

The amounts you have calculated so far are in today's dollars. You must project them into future dollars—what they will be when you retire. Select your Retirement Income Factor from the Retirement Income Table on the facing page and complete the calculations below.

$_____   ×   _____   =   \$_____

| Retirement income you will need in today's dollars (from D) | Retirement Income Factor (from Table II) | [E] Projected annual income at retirement |

This figure represents your annual income at retirement. To figure out the total amount of capital you will need to achieve it, select your Rate of Return Factor from the Rate of Return Table on the facing page, based on what you believe will be a reasonable rate of return on your capital during retirement. Then complete the calculation below.

$_____   ×   _____   =   \$_____

| Projected annual income at retirement (from E) | Rate of Return Factor (from Table III) | [F] Total capital you will need in future dollars |

TABLE 3 Retirement Planning Work Sheet (*Continued*)

II. RETIREMENT INCOME TABLE

Find the number of years closest to your years to retirement. If the exact number of years is not shown, round up to the next higher one. Jot down the Retirement Income Factor from the column that matches your years to retirement. This provides a valuation of your income over time, taking inflation and salary increases into account at a hypothetical rate of 4 percent per year.

Years to retirement	Retirement Income Factor
5	1.22
10	1.48
15	1.80
20	2.19
25	2.67
30	3.23
35	3.95
40	4.80
45	5.84

III. RATE OF RETURN TABLE

Rate of Return	Rate of Return Factor
5%	20.00
6%	16.67
7%	14.29
8%	12.50
9%	11.11
10%	10.00
11%	9.09

TABLE 3 Retirement Planning Work Sheet (*Continued*)

Step 2: What Is Your Retirement Gap?

Your retirement gap is the difference between the capital you have already accumulated and how much you will need on which to live at your desired income level.

Savings and other accounts: Write down the balances of any company retirement accounts, individual retirement accounts, and other retirement accounts you have today. Do not include savings you intend to use for other purposes.

Account   _____ $_____
Account   _____ $_____
Account   _____ $_____
                            Total $_____
                                           [G] Total capital today

Again, you need to calculate what the capital would be worth when you retire. Select your Risk Factor from the Risk Projector Table on the facing page and complete the calculation.

$_____   ×   _____   = $_____

| Total capital today | Risk Factor | [H] Future value of the |
| (from G) | (from Table IV) | capital you have today |

Next, subtract the future value of the capital you have today from the total capital you will need at retirement. This will give you the amount of capital you will have to accumulate during your working years in addition to what you have already accumulated to meet your goal. Remember to factor in the amount you are likely to receive in employer contributions.

$_____   − $_____   = $_____

Total capital you	Future value of	Additional
will need at retire-	the capital you	capital you will need
ment (from F)	have today (from H)	at retirement

TABLE 3 Retirement Planning Work Sheet (*Continued*)

IV. RISK PROJECTOR TABLE

Find your number of years to retirement on the left. Jot down the Risk Factor from the column that matches your tolerance for risk. Assumptions: conservative risk level seeks 7 percent return, moderate risk level seeks 9 percent return, and aggressive risk level seeks 11 percent return.

Years to Retirement	Conservative Risk Factor	Moderate Risk Factor	Aggressive Risk Factor
5	1.40	1.54	1.69
10	1.97	2.37	2.84
15	2.76	3.64	4.78
20	3.87	5.60	8.06
25	5.43	8.62	13.59
30	7.61	13.27	22.89
35	10.68	20.41	38.57
40	14.97	31.41	65.00
45	21.00	48.33	109.53

As you make your way through this work sheet, you must keep in mind that the results can only be approximations, since it is impossible to foretell what the future will bring.

I have based my risk/return levels in the table above on the assumption that you will be *investing* your money rather than merely *saving* it. While historical evidence can never be used to project future results, it can be a guide. I believe the long-term stock market performance I have discussed in the text will support these expectations for conservative, moderate, and aggressive growth rates.

Once you have estimated how much capital you must accumulate for a financially secure retirement, your financial advisor can provide various alternatives for accumulating it.

TABLE 4 How Long Will Your Assets Last?

Withdrawal rate	Growth rate					
	8%	9%	10%	11%	12%	13%
9%	28					
10%	21	26				
11%	17	20	24			
12%	14	16	19	24		
13%	13	14	15	18	23	
14%	11	13	13	15	17	21
15%	10	10	11	13	14	17
16%	9	9	10	11	12	14
17%	9	9	9	10	11	12
18%	8	8	8	9	10	11
19%	7	8	8	8	9	10
20%	7	7	7	8	8	9

The numbers in the table indicate the approximate number of years your assets will last at various growth rates and withdrawal rates when the withdrawal rate is greater than the growth rate. Withdrawal rates are not adjusted for inflation.

Index